THE ANGLICAN QUILT:

Resolving the Anglican crisis over homosexuality

Robert Van de Weyer

BOOKS

Winchester, UK
Washington, USA

THE ANGLICAN QUILT:

Resolving the Anglican crisis over homosexuality

Forewords by:

Most Rev Dr Josiah Idowu-Fearon, Archbishop of
Kaduna, Nigeria, and member of the
Eames Commission

Rt Rev Michael Ingham, Bishop of
New Westminster, Canada

Copyright © 2004 O Books
46A West Street, Alresford, Hants SO24 9AU, U.K.
Tel: +44 (0) 1962 736880 Fax: +44 (0) 1962 736881
E-mail: office@johnhunt-publishing.com
www.O-books.net

U.S.A. and Canada
Books available from :
NBN
15200 NBN Way
Blue Ridge Summit, PA 17214, U.S.A.
Tel: 1 800 462 6420
Fax: 1 800 462 6420
Email: custserv@nbnbooks.com

Text: © Robert Van de Weyer 2004

Design: Graham Whiteman
Text set in ITC Usherwood and Serif Gothic

Cover design: Krave Design, London, UK

ISBN 1 903816 89 0

A CIP catalogue record for this book is available from the British Library.

Printed by Tien Wah Press (Pte) Ltd, Singapore

Endorsements

"A very important contribution."

George Carey, former Archbishop of Canterbury

"A well-thought out explanation with recommendations of the rift that threatens the Anglican Communion worldwide ... sensible and convincing ... profound, academic and thorough."

Josiah Idowu-Fearon, Archbishop of Kaduna, Nigeria, and member of the Eames Commission

"Stimulating, controversial, and full of good sense, as I would expect."　　*Jack Nicholls, Bishop of Sheffield*

"I am glad you have written this ... I agree that some kind of flying bishops may be necessary."

Hugh Montefiore, former Bishop of Birmingham

"There is much in it to admire ... I have no ready alternative to offer."　　*John Habgood, former Archbishop of York*

"I very much wish you well as you seek to reflect upon important issues within the life of the Church at this time."

David Hope, Archbishop of York

"You are addressing very important issues and doing so in a manner which is eminently fair."

James Jones, Bishop of Liverpool

"A very useful contribution, and I think I may well be in agreement with your main conclusions."

Jeffrey John, briefly unconsecrated Bishop of Reading

"I find it both persuasive and stimulating."

Anthony Howard, Times columnist, broadcaster, and commentator on Church of England affairs

"The homosexual issue has exposed deep fault-lines within Anglicanism. The author analyses these, and offers solutions that are far preferable to schism and strife."

William Frend, retired professor of ecclesiastical history at Glasgow University

"It should be read by everybody who cares about the future of the Anglican Church … an alternative strategy to schism that could prevent the Anglican Church from committing suicide."

Nicholas Stacey, clergyman and former deputy director of Oxfam

"A cogently argued and well-worked proposal … this path seems attractive."

Fraser Watts, clergyman and director of the Psychology and Christianity Project

"It is, as everyone would expect, a clear sighted, trenchant and fearless examination of the plight of the Anglican Communion."

Pamela Tudor-Craig, retired professor of the history of art

"Your thoughts will be shared with the Commission."

Robin Eames, Archbishop of Armagh and chairman of the Eames Commission

CONTENTS

Foreword

By Most Rev Dr Josiah Idowu-Fearon, Archbishop of Kaduna Province, Nigeria, and member of the Eames Commission

This is a well-thought out explanation, with recommendations, for the rift that threatens the Anglican Communion worldwide. A large part of the work focuses on the historical origins of the differences in belief and practice among Anglicans, explaining the divide between Evangelicals and the group referred to here as Incarnationals through their respective theology, morality and ecclesiology. The way each group views human issues, though Bible-based, has different slants and approaches. It is as a result of their ways of viewing biblical truth that makes Incarnationals accept homosexuality, while Evangelicals reject it.

The author, therefore, suggests that, rather than the Anglican Church rupturing over such differences, an acceptable compromise should be reached which allows each group to operate its belief system, by allowing separate episcopates. He uses the image of the "quilt" to describe this unity. In the final chapter he breaks down in specific terms the *modus operandi* of this parallel episcopal oversight, covering areas such as law, bishops, church government, selection and training of clergy, finance, buildings, ecumenism, and so on.

From the suggestions made in these four areas of church life, it is obvious that the writer considers the current rift in the Anglican Church irreconcilable, and has therefore made provisions for each group – the Evangelicals and the

Incarnationals – to survive to a great degree independently. The linking factor is church law, which provides the common framework; and a commission would be established to consider legal changes that may be required in the future to accommodate each group.

With such freedom allowed to each group, the link could prove fragile, so that, unless it was managed circumspectly, the "quilt" might disintegrate into total schism. The author's suggestion, under the heading of "ecumenism", that each group should be allowed to form closer bonds, and even merge, with other religious groups is, in my opinion, a potential source of schism.

The writer's arguments sound sensible and convincing, especially as he advocates continued unity, albeit in diversity. However, I believe that the issues of divergence may continue to crop up and grow, as people see the Anglican Church as no different from the world – a place where anything goes. This may mean loss of control, with congregations introducing hitherto unacceptable practices into church, including perhaps in some places witchcraft, polygamy, and the like. Where do we draw the line? What do we do with the teachings and examples of Christ that make us his followers? What do we make of such teachings that tell us not to be conformed to the world, but to be transformed? These questions must not be put aside, as they are central to the debate.

Although I may not agree with the author on all counts, I concede that his contribution to the on-going debate about sexuality in the Church is profound, academic and thorough, and will no doubt be an invaluable source of reflection, information and reference. Its recommendations should form a useful contribution to the search for peace and stability within the worldwide Anglican Communion.

January 28th, 2004

Foreword

By Rt Rev Michael Ingham, Bishop of New Westminster, Vancouver

Current strains within the Anglican Communion over homosexuality are, as Robert van de Weyer rightly argues, merely the tip of a deeper iceberg. From its beginning, Anglican Christianity has sought a unique identity characterized by theological diversity within a common ecclesiastical order. It has been an uneasy compromise at best. In practice, theological consensus has had a lower value in Anglican tradition than institutional structure. We are not a confessional church, as others are, but a liturgical church. We embrace each other within a tradition of common prayer. In the "Faith and Order" equation, we have been rather stronger on the side of order.

The living memory of most Anglican worshipers today extends back barely to the 1950s, a post-war time when churches (in the Western world at least) were often full and played a vital part in community life. Few Anglicans have any serious grasp of the historical turmoils through which Anglican ethos has been formed, still less of the growth and indigenization of Anglican identity in different cultures throughout the world. Nevertheless, we are familiar with the recent controversies over such things as divorce and re-marriage, abortion, and the ordination of women. We have experienced a church that can both adapt to change and also remain historically and biblically grounded. And so the sudden precipitation of our church into possible schism over the issue of homosexuality has caught many Anglicans by surprise.

One of the differences between the current dispute and earlier ones is the existence of the Internet. Modern telecommunications have shrunk the world, and the Anglican Communion, to the point where a word spoken half the globe away can be instantly read and interpreted almost everywhere else - even in time zones that precede the one in which the original utterance occurred. A product of our individualized Western culture, the Internet is a new form of globalization in which common political interests can become aligned very rapidly across international boundaries, and this is no less so within the church. The sexuality debate has become internationalized and also politicized, but without the benefit of the kind of personal knowledge church leaders used to have of each other in a simpler time. Thus, the greater part of the theological iceberg remains largely undetected and invisible to many of its dogmatic combatants.

Amidst the miasma of half-truths and false characterizations promoted by Internet warriors and party lobbyists, there is a great need for clear thinking, historical reflection and Christian charity. Robert Van de Weyer offers these to us in this short book. I write as one who would not agree with all his conclusions, but as one who is nonetheless grateful for the style, tone and nature of his contribution. Theological discussion, even passionate debate, ought to be an enjoyable exercise, a searching after truth, a deepening of friendships. In recent years within the Anglican Church, however, it has become a grim and humorless affair mostly to do with the struggle for power. The notion of a quilt, the central paradigm advanced in this book, is infinitely preferable to the schism being advanced today by some so-called defenders of "orthodoxy."

I have learned a number of things through my own small involvement in this current debate. One is that there are more than two sides to it. In the diocese I serve there are many who would describe themselves, in Van de Weyer's terms, as "evangelical incarnationalists" and vice versa. The use of labels to clarify and distinguish can be a useful tool pedagogically, but it may still fail to satisfy the self-understanding of those for whom relationships remain more important than issues.

From a Canadian perspective, the Church of England's experiment with "flying bishops" seems to be part of the problem rather than part of the solution. Far from weaving the quilt, it appears to have entrenched division and institutionalized separation. Proposals for parallel jurisdictions at the level of bishops will inevitably have a trickle down effect to the point where we would eventually have to appoint parallel incumbents for those in the parish who disagree with the rector. It is a slippery slope to absurdity.

I belong to that (traditionalist) school of thought that believes the structures of Anglicanism to be adequate to the present challenges. The "dissenting minorities" about whom the Primates are rightly concerned - though there are many of them on all sides of this question - are actually protected by the current structures of the church. There is a greater likelihood that parallel jurisdictions will weaken the position of minorities, not safeguard them. In any case, nothing would be left of the historic episcopate if bishops become wandering leaders of theological parties instead of shepherds to their geographic flock.

Perhaps the quilt we need to weave is one of greater theological sophistication and mutual understanding. The frame on which the quilt rests should be left intact.

February 4th, 2004

Acknowledgements

I sent the first draft of this book to various people for comment. I have reviewed these comments in the Afterword. I should like to thank especially David Edwards, William Frend, John Habgood, Richard Kirker, Jeremy Martineau, John Saxbee, Nicholas Stacey and Pamela Tudor-Craig for their detailed critiques.

I also wish to thank Alex and his mother Valerie, in whose coffee shop on Round Church Street in Cambridge much of the book was written, and whose warm welcome is always an encouragement.

Introduction

It seems that the Anglican Church is facing the gravest crisis since its formation almost half a millennium ago. And in October 2003 the primates of the Anglican provinces gathered at Lambeth, at the invitation of the Archbishop of Canterbury, to respond. At the conclusion of their two-day meeting they issued a statement saying that they had requested the Archbishop of Canterbury to appoint a Commission looking into the future of Anglicanism; and the Commission should report back to them in 12 months. A week later the members of the Commission were announced, with Robin Eames, the Irish primate renowned for his "divine optimism," at its head; as many have remarked, he and his fellow commissioners will also need the divine wisdom of Solomon.

The crisis was precipitated by three events. First, Michael Ingham, Bishop of New Westminster in Canada, blessed a homosexual union, and subsequently authorized a rite for such blessings. Secondly, a priest in a longstanding homosexual partnership, Jeffrey John, was appointed suffragan bishop of Reading in England; then under pressure from Evangelicals, and subsequently from the Archbishop of Canterbury, he was persuaded to resign before his consecration. Thirdly, another priest in a homosexual partnership, Gene Robinson, was elected diocesan bishop of New Hampshire in the USA; and despite the open disapproval of the Archbishop of Canterbury, Gene Robinson was duly consecrated on November 2nd, 2003. However, the primates implicitly acknowledged that the issue of homosexuality lies at the surface of a division within Anglicanism that involves every aspect of Christian faith and practice. So they asked that the Commission's "remit be extended to include urgent and deep theological and legal reflection." As Robin Eames made clear in subsequent interviews, the fruit of the Commission's labors should be proposals that both preserve the unity of Anglicanism, while allowing for the differences within it.

If the Anglican Church were a democratic state, then the Commission's proposals would take the form of a consultation document. This would be followed by several months during which the proposals would be openly debated, and members of the public could send in their views; then the executive arm of government would consider these views, and emerge with a draft statute that it would submit to the legislative arm. But in fact the Anglican Church consists of a large number of autonomous provinces scattered across the world. So formal public consultation is impractical, and legislation is impossible. Besides, events are moving too rapidly, and feelings are running too high, for such a ponderous process.

As a result consultation is necessarily more informal and haphazard. No doubt the Eames Commission is fully and acutely aware of the variety of attitudes already expressed across the Anglican Church; and I presume various individuals and organizations will be submitting their ideas directly to the Commission. After the Commission has completed its report, the various recommendations and options contained within it will be eagerly discussed, and perhaps some kind of consensus will emerge. Then the provinces will formally decide what action, if any, they should take. This book is written both as a submission to the Eames Commission, and as a contribution to the subsequent discussion. At the time of writing it contains, to my knowledge, the only detailed plan for resolving the crisis.

The first chapter consists of ten proposals for the Anglican Church as a whole; the first four are statements of fact and principle, the next four are statements of policy, and the last two reflect on long-term implications. It should be said that these last two proposals were written in response to comments made respectively by John Saxbee, Bishop of Lincoln, and Josiah Idowu-Fearon, Archbishop of Kaduna. Indeed, the archbishop's comments are contained in the Foreword. The next three chapters explore the background of these proposals in terms of theology, morality and ecclesiology. The final chapter contains thirteen proposals specifically for the Church of England, which are in effect applications of the eight main proposals. As the mother church of Anglicanism, and as England's national church, the Church of England has unique features; but these proposals are also likely to have relevance to several other provinces.

In the course of preparing the book I engaged in a debate within myself, as a result of which I changed my mind. I was initially stimulated by the excellent foreword to the new edition of *The Way Forward* by Stephen Sykes, a professor of theology and a former bishop of Ely. This book, first published in 1997, is a collection of essays on homosexuality, and its contributors include Jeffrey John and Rowan Williams. Stephen Sykes, writing in July 2003, is convinced that the mutual antagonism of the two sides is so strong that some kind of schism is highly likely, either *de facto* or *de jure*. Reflecting on Stephen Sykes' analysis I concluded that *de jure* schism might also be desirable, and wrote almost an entire book promoting this. But eventually I realized that the arguments were pointing in a somewhat different direction, and I wrote an entirely different book – this one. Its thrust is that the Anglican Church can and should remain intact, but should have in some provinces a parallel episcopal structure similar to that instituted in England when the decision was made to ordain women to the priesthood; and I have used the image of a "quilt" to describe this. Having completed this second draft, I have convinced myself that a quilt is far preferable to schism, and that becoming a quilt is the only realistic way of avoiding schism. I hope I can convince you.

I should add a caveat. The proposals in the first and last chapters, and the discussion in the middle three chapters, are closely connected, but not mutually dependent. The middle chapters offer detailed arguments to justify the quilt proposals, and you might find yourself disagreeing with some or all of these arguments. Yet the proposals could be justified by different arguments; indeed, in my view they commend themselves to straightforward common sense. And in the present crisis it is the proposals that matter.

I should also add a terminological point. For reasons I cannot quite fathom, I have always disliked the term "Anglican Communion." Perhaps it seems to me a little contrived and even slightly precious. So in this book I have used "Anglican Church" instead to describe the whole body of Anglicans throughout the world, and I have distinguished this clearly from the Church of England.

Finally I want to thank the two distinguished Anglican leaders who have written a foreword to this book. Both are men of deep thought and sterling courage. Josiah Idowu-

Fearon is archbishop in the country that now boasts the largest Anglican community in the world, and hence wields great influence in Anglican affairs. Michael Ingham is either one of the heroes or one of the villains of the present crisis in Anglicanism, depending on one's point of view. I am pleased that, while welcoming this book, they are also critical of some aspects of it. I am doubly pleased that their grounds for criticism are so different. Bishop Michael rightly says that discussion and debate amongst Christians should be enjoyable and friendly, and regrets that much of the current debate is "grim and humorless." If this book helps to inject a little joy and warmth into the crisis, then it will have served a valuable purpose.

CHAPTER 1:

PROPOSALS FOR THE WHOLE ANGLICAN CHURCH

Concerning names

It is clear to outside observers of the Anglican Church, as well as those within it, that the present division is simple in that there are only two sides. But there is considerable muddle about the appropriate names, and this muddle betrays uncertainty about the underlying beliefs that those on each side hold. So we must find names that are accurate. They must also be respectful, such that those on each side are happy to be identified by them.

Journalists and other outside commentators frequently call those on one side "traditionalists" or "conservatives", and those on the other "modernizers" or "liberals." Yet these terms are highly misleading. In the first place many "traditionalists" have in recent decades been remarkably innovative and imaginative in their styles of worship, while many "modernizers" are quite conservative in their liturgical tastes. Secondly, those on the "liberal" side generally have firm and often quite strict views; they are simply somewhat different from those that outsiders habitually associate with Christianity. Thirdly, the religious convictions of both sides have deep roots in Anglican history, and so both can justly claim to be traditional. Indeed, one party traces its ancestry to the Puritans of the late 16th century, although John Wesley is probably its pivotal figure. The other party looks back to Richard Hooker and others like him who defended the so-called Elizabethan settlement.

In the light of their ancestry it is tempting to call one party Wesleyan and the other party Hookerite; but the former name has long been associated with one stream of Methodism, while the latter is too obscure. Instead, I propose that one party be called "Evangelical," which is a term that has been in widespread use for around two centuries. Members of that party are generally happy to use it about themselves – although some, in the conviction that they form the mainstream of Anglicanism, wish to drop any kind of party label. Finding a term for the other party is more problematic, since there is no term in current or past usage that is either precise or well-known – largely, perhaps, because views within the party have been more fluid. However, I suggest that the name "Incarnational" is appropriate; and this too would, I believe, be regarded with favor by many of those identified by it.

The basic difference between the two parties is epistemological, and the epistemological difference justifies their respective names. For Evangelicals the foundation of all religious truth is the Bible, which is the unique and complete divine revelation. For Incarnationals the foundation is human experience, in which divinity is apprehended and through which it is inferred. Evangelicals do not deny the importance of experience, but interpret experience as confirming biblical testimony. Conversely, Incarnationals place great importance on the Bible and the whole Christian tradition, but use the Bible and tradition to inspire and inform experience – and they claim that the Bible actually encourages this approach. Thus for Evangelicals Christianity imparts the divine message – the evangel. For Incarnationals Christianity shows how divinity truth is embodied in human life – how it is incarnate.

Books about the Anglican Church have generally presented it as a coalition between three parties, rather than two, and these have been called "high church," "low church," and "broad church." In relation to these names, Evangelicals are "low," while Incarnationals can most readily be termed "broad." This raises the question of where "high" churchmen – or "Anglo-Catholics" as they have been more usually called since the late 19th century – fit into the epistemological picture. As doctrinal debates in recent decades have demonstrated, Evangelicals and Anglo-Catholics share a great deal of common theological ground. Like Evangelicals, traditional Anglo-Catholics generally regard the Bible as the foundation of religious truth; and they differ only in the greater importance they attach to the creeds formulated by the early church – but they readily acknowledged these as interpretations of Biblical revelation. However, there are now a significant number of "liberal" Anglo-Catholics, who relish Anglo-Catholic liturgical styles, but whose doctrinal approach is distinctly Incarnational. Thus the Anglo-Catholic element within Anglicanism has become doctrinally divided – although the majority is undoubtedly closer to Evangelical than to Incarnational epistemology. It should also be noted that the number of Anglo-Catholics, especially in England, has declined rapidly in the past 30 years or so.

These reflections on the position of Anglo-Catholicism indicate a drawback in the term "Evangelical." A more accurate alternative would be "Orthodox," as this would more clearly include Evangelicals and (non-liberal) Anglo-Catholics. I suggest that the Eames Commission seriously considers this. For the purposes of the present book, however, I stick to "Evangelical" for two reasons. First, "Orthodox" for most people continues to signify "Eastern Orthodox," and this could only be changed by the Eames Commission itself bringing the term into Anglican usage. Secondly, the vast majority of Anglicans across the world are familiar with "Evangelical" as indicating Bible-based Christian doctrine.

This bald epistemological summary of the two main Anglican positions is inevitably rather abstract and simplistic. In the following chapters I shall outline the ways in which these differing epistemologies have shaped Evangelical and Incarnational ideas in the three main areas of Christian belief: theology, morality and ecclesiology. I hope readers in each party will recognize their own convictions in these outlines, and also perhaps understand a little better the convictions of those in the other party.

Thus, the first proposal to the Commission is:

> *It is recognized that there are distinct approaches to Christian faith and practice within the Anglican Church that may be called Evangelical (or Orthodox) and Incarnational.*

Concerning difference

Since the present crisis began there has been much talk in Anglican circles about "schism", with some actively promoting it, some regretting it but regarding it as inevitable, and some strongly opposing it. Yet, since both parties have existed since the birth of Anglicanism, we must ask why their differences have now become so sharp and bitter.

The reason is that in the past their contrasting epistemologies actually led to theological, moral and ecclesiological convictions bearing a close resemblance to one another; but in recent decades the face of Incarnationalism has changed quite noticeably. The most significant change, of course, concerns moral thought, which has altered Incarnational attitudes to homosexuality. Until about a century ago Incarnationals continued to subscribe to the medieval idea of natural law, which forbids homosexual relations, and this accorded with the biblical injunctions against homosexuality that guided Evangelical attitudes. But for good, rational reasons most Incarnationals have now abandoned natural law theory, and adopted a somewhat different understanding of the relations between nature and morality; and their new understanding is generally positive to committed homosexual partnerships.

As many on both sides have recognized, this divergence on morality is closely related to, and symptomatic of, an important theological shift. Natural law morality arose out a view of God as the designer of the world as it exists, ordaining laws to govern how it functions, and moral laws are a subset of these. But scientific advances have compelled many Incarnational thinkers to abandon this notion of divinity, and instead to pay far closer attention to the ways in which the human mind actually discerns and conceives of divinity. And just as the issue of homosexuality has exposed the moral divide between Evangelicals and Incarnationals, so our growing awareness of the other religions of the world has helped to expose these theological differences, with Evangelicals regarding all other religions as theologically wrong, and Incarnationals searching them for theological insights. There is a corresponding divergence in ecclesiology, and this is being exposed, in the West at least, by the differing responses to the challenge of decline in formal religious affiliation.

In outlining Evangelical and Incarnational theology, morality and ecclesiology in the following chapters, I shall seek to show in more depth how the gap between their respective ideas has widened. This will indicate that the gap is now so wide that Evangelical and Incarnational Anglicans need a degree of separation from one another – greater than the present arrangements allow. And with a greater degree of separation, and the freedom that it will confer, Evangelical and Incarnational Anglicanism will both be better able to flourish.

Therefore the second proposal is:

It is recognized that the difference between Evangelical

and Incarnational Anglican convictions has increased in recent times, and that disagreement concerning homosexuality has arisen as a result of this.

Concerning unity

While the differences between the two parties is greater than ever before, it would be foolish to deny that there has been bitter conflict in the past. Indeed, their mutual antipathy helped to fuel the English Civil War, with the Evangelicals (or, more precisely, their Puritan forbears) siding with the Parliamentarians, and the Incarnationals tending to side with the Royalists. And at various times groups from each party have become so frustrated at having to co-exist with the other party that they have broken away. The most important such split occurred when many of John Wesley's followers, after his death, decided to turn Methodism into a separate "connection."

Nonetheless, the Anglican Church has somehow held together, with many people, both within and outside it, admiring its "comprehensiveness". Its survival must surely count as one of the more remarkable miracles of Christian history. So we should ask whether, despite the current differences, there is value in trying to sustain the miracle into the future.

A positive answer lies in their respective epistemologies. Since the time of John Wesley Evangelical Anglicans have regarded personal experiences as confirmation of the truth of the Bible. In fact, the relevance of personal experiences was central to the disagreement between Wesley and the Puritans. And the Charismatic movement, which has profoundly influenced modern

Anglican Evangelicalism, lays even greater stress on experience. Conversely, Incarnationals would not be Christian were it not for their attachment to the Bible. There are Incarnational versions of other religions, most notably Hinduism and Taoism; and arguably those of mystical inclination in every religion are liable to be Incarnational in their thinking. It is also possible to be Incarnational without belonging to any religious tradition. The distinctiveness of Incarnational Christians is that their convictions are shaped by the gospel of Christ.

Thus although Evangelicals and Incarnationals have different epistemological foundations, the theological, moral and ecclesiastical edifices built on those foundations touch at important points, and in the following chapters I shall try to demonstrate this. Surprisingly the two edifices even touch on the issue of homosexuality. In seeking to justify their opposition to homosexual relations, Evangelicals do not just quote the Bible, but they also appeal to scientific evidence about the nature of homosexual orientation – that it may in some cases be a matter of choice, that it may be changed by various kinds of psychological therapy, and so on. Conversely, in seeking to explain their approval of committed homosexual partnerships, Incarnationals try to show that their approval conforms to the overall spiritual and moral message of the Bible. So although the two parties may never agree, the nature of the arguments has much in common, and this suggests that continuing dialogue may be helpful.

The term "schism" is a metaphor, deriving from the Greek word for "tear" – as in "tearing a piece of cloth." Just as tearing cloth in two loosens and weakens the weave, so tearing Evangelical and Incarnational Anglicanism apart may cause profound damage to them both. The alternative to schism, in which they have greater distance from one another and yet remain united, can be expressed in a related and more homely metaphor: that of a quilt. A quilt consists of two pieces of cloth held apart by padding, and held together by stitching. And a quilt, of course, has the advantage of being much warmer than a single piece of cloth.

Therefore, the third proposal to the Commission is:

It is recognized that both Evangelical and Incarnational Anglicans benefit in their Christian faith and practice by belonging to a single ecclesiastical entity.

Concerning provinces

The provinces of the Anglican Church vary greatly in their proportions of Evangelical and Incarnational members.

In provinces where Anglicanism arose through the work of missionaries from England, the form depends crucially on the allegiance of the missionary society that sent them. Incarnational Anglicans were the pioneers, with the formation of SPG in 1701. But the most effective society, formed almost a century later, was CMS, which was strongly Evangelical. And most of the smaller societies founded during the 19th century were also Evangelical. As a result Evangelicalism holds sway through much of the Anglican Church in Africa and Asia.

Outside observers of the present dispute have frequently described it as being between "north" and "south," or, worse still, between "rich" and "poor." And Anglicans must surely shudder at the thought that their

Church may divide along lines of relative wealth. This has nasty echoes of the division within the Corinthian church that Paul strived to heal. But in fact the description is quite wide of the mark. The truth is that in about one third of the Anglican provinces there are substantial numbers of both Evangelicals and Incarnationals, and in about two-thirds of the provinces Evangelicalism dominates. Thus in order to resolve the dispute in Anglicanism as a whole, a means must be found of resolving the dispute within the third of provinces where Evangelicals and Incarnationals exist side by side.

This leads to the fourth proposal:

> It is recognized that maintaining the unity of the Anglican Church as a whole depends on finding a satisfactory means of maintaining unity in those provinces where there are substantial numbers of both Evangelical and Incarnational Anglicans.

Concerning episcopacy

According to Anglican tradition the foci of unity are the bishops, and bishops sustain unity by means of authorizing and supervising the ministry within local congregations. Thus the primary symptom of disunity in the present crisis is individual churches refusing to accept the authority and supervision of their local bishop, and seeking episcopal oversight from elsewhere.

In principle there is no need to have a single bishop for each area, and hence there is no objection to different churches in an area having different bishops. The firm connection between episcopacy and geography certainly has no biblical basis, and probably arose as the church sought to model itself on the Roman civil administration. The challenge in the present crisis is to find some means of allowing congregations to choose the kind of bishop that accords with their convictions, while preserving some kind of unified structure.

Happily the dilemma over the ordination of women in England provides a valuable precedent. Congregations adamantly opposed to women priests were permitted to have the oversight of a bishop that shared their view. In fact, two bishops were appointed, one to function in the north of the country and one in the south; and since the number of congregations opting for their oversight was quite small, two bishops proved quite enough. A special law was drafted and passed to ensure that they remained firmly within the Anglican structure.

The limitation of this precedent is that it relates to a single issue, whereas the present dispute, while the single issue of homosexuality is at the fore, is far deeper and more complex. In this regard a much older precedent is relevant. Since the 12th century the Roman Catholic Church has established a number of "uniat" churches in areas where various eastern churches are predominant. These uniat churches are allowed to maintain their own liturgies and canon law, and have their own bishops, while at the same time being in full communion with Rome. And their episcopal structures function in parallel with the normal "Latin" episcopate. Thus each area typically has two bishops, one uniat and one Latin, and they oversee their respective congregations. Admittedly the uniat churches submit to Rome on basic matters of faith and morals, but they mostly retain their distinct theological outlook, and have a distinct ethos. Several uniat churches, for example, allow priests to marry.

Although it may be possible to define the basic difference between Evangelical and Incarnational Anglicanism in precise epistemological terms, most practicing Anglicans do not think in these terms, nor do they reflect too deeply on their own theological, moral and ecclesiological beliefs; so they might be uncertain as to whether they are Evangelical or Incarnational. In fact, the issue of homosexuality, as I have indicated, acts as a useful test, since it correlates closely with people's convictions as a whole. Thus if a congregation is willing to receive the ministry of a priest in a homosexual partnership, provided that the priest is suitable in other ways, then it would be right for that congregation to have an Incarnational bishop. If not, then the congregation should have an Evangelical bishop.

Thus the fifth proposal is:

> *Each province in the Anglican Church should deter-mine whether its membership is overwhelmingly unified in its convictions, or whether it has signifi-cant numbers of both Evangelical and Incarnational members. Those in the latter category should have both Evangelical and Incarnational bishops, and congregations should be free to choose which type of episcopal authority to accept. In being offered this choice, congregations may be asked whether they would ever be willing to accept the ministry of a priest who is in a homosexual partnership.*

Congregations giving a positive answer would be offered Incarnational episcopal oversight.

Concerning ministry

While bishops are the foci and sustainers of unity, communion is its primary expression and symbol. Thus for Anglicans, as for most Christians, disunity consists first and foremost in the breaking of communion. This has two quite distinct aspects within the present Anglican context. First, individuals in one party may refuse to have communion with those in the other party. Secondly, ordained ministers of one party may not be permitted to exercise their ministry in churches associated with the other party.

Most Anglicans would surely regard the first aspect as a matter of personal conscience. It is a biblical requirement that the sharing of communion should only occur where there is genuine fellowship; and individuals must be the ultimate judges of this. Indeed, I am not aware of any discussion in either party about imposing on individuals some kind of corporate discipline in this regard.

The second aspect, however, is more problematic. At present there is a general understanding within the Anglican Church that priests from one diocese or province are allowed to minister in other dioceses and provinces, provided they are in "good standing." So any restriction on this freedom of movement would be a significant change. Yet there can be little doubt that such a change is now inevitable. Indeed, Archbishop Williams has already indicated that Bishop Gene Robinson of New Hampshire would probably be refused a license to minister in England.

And if, as I have proposed, some provinces have both Evangelical and Incarnational bishops, then it seems unlikely that bishops of one party will readily grant licenses to priests under the jurisdiction of a bishop of another party.

While at first sight this might seem sad, it will not in practice cause much disruption, since few priests will want to move about in this way. The important issue is how this restriction is implemented. Inevitably if an entire province, or the bench of bishops of one party within a province, declares itself out of communion with another province or bench, this will be seen, both within and outside the Anglican Church, as a serious blow to unity. Besides, this kind of provincial declaration is contrary to the custom and tradition of Anglicanism – and may be illegal. Anglicans have always regarded the licensing of priests as a matter for individual bishops, using their own judgment and discretion; and this is how it should remain.

Thus the sixth proposal is:

> *It should be a matter for individual bishops to determine which ordained ministers might exercise a ministry in the churches in their oversight.*

Concerning Canterbury

The unity of the worldwide Anglican Church is traditionally understood in terms of the position of the Archbishop of Canterbury. All the provinces, and all the members of all the provinces, are in communion with him. Clearly, if there are to be parallel episcopates, this has serious implications for his position. To use the metaphor of this book's title, he will come to symbolize the stitching that holds the two cloths together. It is vital, therefore, that the Archbishop of

Canterbury is someone who is sympathetic with, and respectful of, both the Evangelical and the Incarnational parties, and is by and large acceptable to both.

This is not as hard as it may sound. The present incumbent, Rowan Williams, both through his writings and through his actions as a bishop in Wales, showed himself supportive of the ministry of priests in homosexual partnerships. But after a wobbly start at Canterbury, he quickly realized that the office required him to work in harmony with Evangelical opinion. And any future incumbent, regardless of his personal views, would surely follow his example.

Since the worldwide Anglican Church is overwhelmingly Evangelical, it would clearly be wise normally to appoint people to Canterbury who were themselves Evangelical, or at least "orthodox" in the sense that I used the term earlier. And from my own experience in Africa – and I hope that the next Archbishop of Canterbury is African – I know personally several bishops who are strongly Evangelical in their convictions, and yet who have the breadth of understanding and intellect that would enable them to embrace Incarnationals as well.

Thus the seventh proposal is:

> *Those responsible for the appointment of the Archbishop of Canterbury should ensure that the person has sympathy with both Evangelical and Incarnational convictions. For the foreseeable future persons appointed to this office should be Evangelical, recognizing that the great majority of members of the worldwide Anglican Church is Evangelical.*

Concerning ecumenism

One of the most remarkable developments within
Anglicanism in recent decades has been the recognition
that individual provinces can merge with other Christian
denominations, while remaining fully part of the Anglican
fold. The pioneer of such ecumenism was the Church of
South India, inaugurated in 1947, in which the Anglican
Church joined with the Methodist Church and several
Reformed churches. The Church of England herself almost
followed the Indian example in the late 1960s, when it
negotiated a scheme for unity with the English Methodists.
The only major proviso is that the merged denomination
should have episcopal government.

Those devoted to the cause of ecumenism may look
upon the present dispute within Anglicanism with alarm,
fearing that it may result in a major setback. In fact, it
could – and should – be the springboard for a major
advance. Currently an important stumbling block to
ecumenism is that Evangelical and Incarnational Anglicans
want closer relations with different kinds of churches.
Indeed, in 1970, when the Anglican-Methodist scheme
finally came to the vote, Evangelicals played a major role in
defeating it, partly out of fears that modern English
Methodism is too Incarnational. But if Evangelicals and
Incarnationals had distinct episcopal structures, then this
stumbling block would be removed – since each would be
able to forge alliances and negotiate mergers as they
pleased. I can imagine, for example, many free Evangelical
congregations actually wanting to come under the Anglican
Evangelical wing, as they would enjoy many practical
advantages. And it is quite possible that a new Anglican-

Methodist scheme could be devised and agreed.

Thus the eighth proposal is:

> *In provinces where there are both Evangelical and Incarnational episcopal structures, those in each should be free to seek great unity, and even merge, with non-Anglican churches sharing their respective convictions, provided that an episcopal structure is maintained.*

Concerning precedents

The notion of separate episcopates for Evangelicals and Incarnationals – albeit in only some of the Anglican provinces – raises the question of whether any group or party within Anglicanism, which happens to have a particular doctrinal conviction distinct from the mainstream, could have its own episcopate. As already noted, those opposed to women priests within England have their own separate episcopal arrangements; and, in order to allow the appointment of women bishops, there is even a proposal for the formation of a separate "men-only" province for those implacably opposed to such a development. One can readily envisage other issues, currently bubbling just below the surface of public awareness, rising to prominence in the future. For example, there are many Evangelicals who feel very uneasy about infant baptism, and would prefer to confine baptism to believers. And there is a growing number of Incarnationals exploring the implications of a "non-real" conception of God. Eventually, there could be a multiplicity of different episcopates, each representing a particular religious position, and parishes would choose between them.

There are three reasons why this would be wrong, and is also unlikely to occur. First, separate episcopal arrangements could only be appropriate where the dispute concerns the type of people entitled to exercise the ordained ministry, and such questions are very limited in number. Indeed, the issue of women priests and bishops, and that of gay priests and bishops, are probably the only such issues that could conceivably arise. By contrast, disputes over such issues as baptism policy could in principle be made matters for individual parishes to decide, while retaining common episcopal supervision. Indeed, Anglicanism already accommodates all kinds of differences in this way.

Secondly, Evangelicals and Incarnationals are the inheritors of the two main traditions that have co-existed within the Anglican Church since its formation, so those with allegiance to one or other of these traditions should properly be allowed to call themselves Anglican. The problem (as I have already noted, and shall explore further) is that in recent decades Incarnationalism has moved away from Evangelicalism, with the issue of homosexual priests and bishops lying at the surface of a more profound division, so they now need separate episcopates. However, supporters of believers-only baptism and non-real theology can make no claim to belonging to an ancient Anglican tradition.

Thirdly, and fundamentally, Evangelicalism and Incarnationalism are, in philosophical terminology, "mutually exclusive and exhaustive." In other words, a Christian of any description is either Evangelical, in the sense of regarding the Bible as the foundation of religious truth, or Incarnational, regarding experience as the ultimate test of truth. By this definition Roman Catholicism and Eastern Orthodoxy are "Evangelical" churches – although the awkwardness of this description gives further weight to the notion of replacing the term "Evangelical" with "Orthodox." By the same token, and acknowledging the same awkwardness, the opponents of women priests and bishops are Evangelical, in that they justify their view primarily on biblical grounds. Incarnational doctrine, by contrast, implies the possibility that the Bible may be wrong, so that its teaching must always be tested against experience. Thus, to take the examples cited earlier, the debate concerning baptism is essentially an Evangelical matter, resting on different interpretations of the Bible. Conversely, openness to the possibility of a non-real understanding of God could only occur within an Incarnational context, since the biblical view of God is robustly real.

Thus the ninth proposal is:

> *Separate episcopal arrangements for Evangelicals and Incarnationals need not, and should not, be regarded as a precedent for separate episcopal arrangements for other groups or parties within the Anglican Church.*

Concerning the future

As Archbishop Idowu-Fearon observes in his Foreword, there is a danger that, once the Evangelicals and Incarnationals have separate episcopates, they may drift apart even more rapidly than they have already been in recent decades. He also expresses the fear that separate episcopates might lead to a weakening of moral and spiritual discipline. Indeed, although he is too gracious to say this explicitly, his anxiety about the development of an "anything goes" mentality probably applies mainly to the Incarnational side.

As matters currently stand, with both sides sharing the same episcopate, they are sufficiently far apart that they must devote considerable energy to defining their differences; and this in turn makes the conflict more acute. Conversely, if they enjoyed the degree of separation that distinct episcopates would allow, this energy would be saved, and tensions reduced. This in turn would allow them, in the fullness of time, to find and explore their points of common interest. In fact, this accords with our common experience of personal relationships. When two siblings or friends, or even a husband and wife, are too close they may start to bicker and argue, but if they have a degree of independence they are often better able to appreciate one another.

The danger of an "anything goes" mentality is already implicit in the way in which authority is devolved within Anglicanism. Throughout Anglican history there have been instances where individual provinces or dioceses have adopted practices of which Anglicans elsewhere have strongly disapproved; but even in the midst of disagreement, the protagonists have usually been able to respect one another's moral and spiritual integrity. The election of Gene Robinson to the bishopric of New Hampshire, and the subsequent ratification by the whole Episcopal Church of the USA, is, of course, a symptom of this devolution of authority; and to some Evangelicals it is also a symptom of moral laxity and decadence. But many Evangelicals, while strongly disapproving of Gene

Robinson's way of life, nonetheless recognize the sincerity of his faith. Were it the case that in due course the majority of Incarnationals became relativist in their morality, lacking any firm principles, then few would doubt that Evangelicals should part company with them entirely; but that is not the case at present, and in my view it is unlikely.

It is quite possible that over the coming years and decades the internal dynamics of Evangelicalism and Incarnationalism will gradually push them further apart, until total schism becomes unavoidable. If that occurs, then the fact that they will already have separate episcopates, and thence be accustomed to running their own affairs as distinct entities, will make the schism far less messy and acrimonious. It is also possible – and I think more likely, for reasons explored in later chapters – that the two sides will gradually draw closer together again, so that the two episcopates will eventually merge. Indeed, John Habgood, former Archbishop of York and architect of the system of flying bishops for those opposed to women priests, has expressed the hope that the two sides in that dispute may in due course be reconciled, so that the flying bishops may return to earth. And it must be the fervent hope and prayer of every Anglican that the present much deeper rift may ultimately be healed.

Thus the tenth and final proposal is:

> *Separate episcopal arrangements for Evangelicals and Incarnationals should not be regarded necessarily as a permanent arrangement. Every Anglican should be enjoined to pray for a time when Evangelicals and Incarnationals are sufficiently close that they can harmoniously share a common episcopacy.*

CHAPTER 2:

THEOLOGY

Evangelical theology: the heart strangely warmed

The Puritans, who formed a vocal and influential minority within the Church of England from almost the moment of its formation, adopted the ideas of John Calvin, the French reformer who sought to turn the city of Geneva into a Protestant paradise. Like all the Protestant reformers, Calvin aimed to base his thought entirely on the Bible. But his theology was distinct in two ways. First, in explaining how Christians know the Bible to be true, Calvin argued that God inserts this knowledge directly into the minds of those whom he intends to save. Secondly, in explaining why some are saved and some not, Calvin asserted that salvation is purely a matter of divine choice – and that God decided whom he would save, and whom he would condemn, before the creation of the world. To Calvin, and to his Puritan followers in England, these doctrines arise from the basic biblical teaching of the supreme power and majesty of God, and any idea that human beings can judge for themselves whether or not the Bible is true, or can do anything to determine whether or not they are saved, is blasphemy.

Born in 1703, John Wesley was the son of the Puritan rector of the Lincolnshire town of Epworth. Yet as a young man Wesley grew to doubt whether he himself had been chosen by God for salvation, and this doubt caused profound mental agony, as he recorded in his *Journal*. Finally, under the influence of the Moravian Brethren – a Protestant church based in central Europe – he came to believe that God offers salvation to all people, allowing each individual to accept or reject it. This divine offer is made through the person of Jesus Christ, so becoming Christian involves embracing Christ as personal savior. Wesley himself accepted Christ as his savior on the evening of May 24th, 1738; and his description of his conversion is a classic text of Evangelical Christianity:

"I felt my heart strangely warmed. I felt I did trust in Christ, Christ alone for salvation; and an assurance was given me that he had taken away my sins, even mine, and saved me from the law of sin and death. ... I was much buffeted with temptations, but cried out and they fled away. They returned again and again. I as often lifted up my eyes and he sent help from his holy place. And herein I found in what the difference between this and my former state chiefly consisted. ... Then I was sometimes, if not often, conquered; now I was always conqueror."

The following year John Wesley set out on the peripatetic mission that was to occupy the rest of his long life, typically preaching five sermons a day to anyone who cared to listen. Having concluded that salvation is a matter of individual choice, he wanted to persuade as many individuals as possible to choose it. So his message was simple: welcome Jesus Christ into your life, and be saved. But as his message, and the theology behind it, became widely known, so many Puritans came to regard him as a heretic. Their main objection was that he was making divine action subject to human whim, and thereby putting humans above God. But some had a subtler, and ultimately more potent, reason for opposing him: his theology destroyed the internal coherence of Calvinism, and thereby undermined its epistemology – its claim to be true.

The nub of this epistemological argument is illustrated in Wesley's own conversion. Wesley became convinced of the genuineness of his salvation as a result of the spiritual experiences following his commitment to Christ: he received a personal assurance that he was now free from sins; and he found that he could defeat every temptation to sin. Until that time Wesley had held an intellectual belief in the truth of the Bible and its message, yet had received no inner sign that this message applied to him; now the strange warmth in his heart melted his doubt. But to the Puritan Wesley's feelings and emotions on that summer evening were insignificant, and possibly dangerous: they were merely subjective, and could have been have been induced by all sorts of stimuli that have no connection with the Bible; they could even have been the work of the Devil. To the Puritan salvation is self-confirming: when individuals are saved, God informs them both that the Bible is truth, and that its truth applies to them. By introducing an element of choice, the Wesleyan theology needs some human indication that the choice is right; but to the Puritan any human indication is unreliable – and hence any human choice is open to question. In effect, Wesley was only making a single hole in the closed epistemological circle of Puritan theology; but to the Puritans even one hole was enough to break it apart.

The conflict between Wesleyan and Puritan theology continued within Anglicanism right into the 20th century. Indeed, when my wife and I came to live in Lancaster in northern England in 1973, St Thomas' Church was still a Puritan redoubt – albeit with a small and diminishing congregation. And I heard some distinctly Puritan sermons in Namirembe Cathedral in Uganda 10 years later. The conflict raged equally fiercely outside the Anglican Church, even within Methodism itself; and in the early 20th century the great German theologian, Karl Barth, produced a theological system with many similarities to Calvinism.

However, in the final decades of the 20th century Wesleyan theology received a huge boost from the Charismatic movement, which shook the entire fabric of Evangelical Anglicanism – even those Evangelical congregations that did not explicitly espouse it. Charismatic theology regards the receiving of a gift from God's Spirit, such as speaking in tongues, as both the fruit and the confirmation of salvation; and since the source of salvation is Jesus Christ as proclaimed in the Bible, the spiritual gifts also confirm the Bible's veracity. The Charismatic movement has in turn influenced the way in which the Bible is interpreted, allowing a far greater degree of freedom than even Wesley, let alone the Puritans, would have permitted. Since God's Spirit is active in the hearts and minds of individuals, the Bible's texts must be understood in the light of that activity; and the activity of the Spirit should lead us to expect fresh insights into the biblical texts, as they apply to today's problems and challenges. Thus Charismatic theology is willing to punch holes at any point in the Puritan circle.

In epistemological terms Evangelical theology may properly be described as pragmatic, in the sense in which the philosopher William James developed the term. According to pragmatism there is a certain type of belief – an "overbelief" – that is beyond what can be verified empirically, and yet may have great importance and value in people's lives. And while certain social, moral and psychological beliefs fall into this category, the most important are religious beliefs. James, therefore, proposes an alternative method of verification: such beliefs may be regarded as true if the consequences of holding them are good. Some Evangelicals and Charismatics may wish to say that their spiritual experiences constitute a direct encounter with God, and therefore are an empirical verification of Christian beliefs. But Wesley certainly did not regard his inner experiences in this light; rather they amounted to an overwhelming sense of divine goodness and love.

Incarnational theology: the divine bosom

Although Richard Hooker was a contemporary of Shakespeare, his *Treatise on the Laws of Ecclesiastical Polity* is notoriously turgid. Nonetheless this scholarly country parson coined a single poetical phrase that set the tone of Incarnational theology within the Anglican Church.

According to Hooker, there is a natural law "whose seat is the bosom of God, her voice the harmony of the world."

A century later John Locke, one of the most remarkable and influential thinkers that England has produced, turned Hooker's metaphors into a coherent religious philosophy. Locke is mainly associated with a form of empiricism known as representative realism, in which sensory perception is regarded as the only foundation for genuine knowledge. However, he had always been a devout Anglican, and towards the end his life, in a book entitled *The Reasonableness of Christianity*, he applied his empiricism to Christian doctrine. His main conclusion was simple: sensory impressions of nature indicate that the different species of the world live in a harmonious relationship with one another, thus their existence must be governed by natural laws that have been ordained by a supreme intelligence. It follows that the laws of nature are also the laws of God. A century later William Paley expressed this inference in a powerful metaphor: just as the elaborate mechanisms of a watch compel us to believe in the existence of a watchmaker, so the infinitely elaborate mechanisms of the universe compel us to believe in God.

The empirical basis of "natural theology," as it came to be called, made it vulnerable to new scientific discoveries. And Charles Darwin's theory of evolution, allied to the theory of genetic inheritance initially formulated by the Austrian monk Gregor Mendel, are now generally taken to discredit Locke and Paley. Indeed, the biologist Richard Dawkins recently danced on Paley's grave by entitling a book *The Blind Watchmaker*. Far from requiring a divine designer, biological harmony has been achieved by a combination of random genetic mutations and natural selection: those mutations that help a species adapt to its environment, and hence give it a better chance of surviving, are passed on to future generations – and this process of mutual adaptation has produced the natural order that we observe. Natural theology is currently enjoying a modest revival, as scientifically minded Christians search for a higher level of divine design in cosmology, and a deeper level in quantum mechanics. Some argue that the cosmos may have been "fine-tuned" to generate intelligent beings, like ourselves, capable of apprehending the tuner. But they admit, unlike Locke and Paley, that at best we can only infer the possibility of God's existence – and that we can never measure the strength of that possibility.

Alongside Locke's empiricism, a strain of thought developed within Anglicanism exploring the way in which human beings can directly experience divinity, and thence participate in the divinity of Christ. Essentially this theology is mystical, and has often drawn inspiration from the great flowering of mysticism in late medieval England – exemplified by such figures as Julian of Norwich and Richard Rolle. Within the post-Reformation Church of England it first received clear expression amongst a group of mystical writers in the mid 17th century who also drew inspiration from early Christian Platonist writers such as Clement of Alexandria – and thus became known as the Cambridge Platonists. For them the great truth of Christianity is that God is love. Thus divine truth is manifest throughout the material order. In the words of Ralph Cudworth, God "enclaspeth the whole world within his outstretched arms, his soul is as wide as the whole universe, as big as yesterday, today and forever." But divine love is fully revealed in the person of Christ; and Christ both invites us to become like him and also offers us the grace to accept this invitation. Thus any and every human being may become an incarnation of God.

Perhaps the most influential exponent of this kind of Incarnational theology was F D Maurice. His formal academic works are even more impenetrable than Hooker's writings, but he expressed himself with remarkable lucidity and passion in the articles he wrote for popular magazines during the middle years of the 19th century, when he was the intellectual leader of the Christian Socialist movement. He strongly opposed those of his fellow Christian socialists who wanted to "build" the kingdom of God on earth, as if God's kingdom were a human creation. The kingdom of God, according to Maurice, is already present in every human heart, and thence in the social structures that individuals naturally tend to create. Thus we should "dig" for the kingdom, helping people to find it within and between themselves. This task of digging is the essence of Christian ministry; and Christian social and political action should consist in giving people the intellectual and economic resources to become effective diggers on their own behalf.

Although Maurice is frequently regarded as a "broad churchman," his views were taken up by more radical high churchman such as Charles Gore, and later by William Temple, who became archbishop of Canterbury during the Second World War. Maurice frequently referred to digging for God's kingdom as "sacramental," in that it is a means of divine grace. Temple adapted this notion to describe the way in which human beings should relate to the natural, as well as the social, order. And it is this line of thinking which in turn has exercised particular appeal over recent decades within the environmental movement. Despite the environmental movement being essentially secular in its aims, a surprising number of its leading advocates subscribe to the idea that all life – human, animal and plant – is essentially an incarnation of divinity. Hence in treating the natural order with respect, cherishing each species within it, human beings are acting in accordance with the divine spirit within them. Indeed, if the Charismatic movement has given fresh impetus to Evangelicalism, so the environmental movement has had a similar effect on Incarnationalism over the same period, and today most Incarnational Anglicans are "green."

While the epistemology of this kind of Incarnationalism is essentially empirical, it is quite different from the empiricism of Locke. In modern terms Locke's empiricism takes the form of "inference to the best explanation," in which the existence of a supreme intelligence is used to explain what is observed in the world. Claims of direct experience of divinity are in the first place matters of psychology, and William James (as a psychologist rather than as a philosopher of pragmatism) remains unsurpassed in his analysis of religious experience. Typically Incarnationals go on to claim that such experiences are actual encounters with God, involving no inference whatever. This was the view of Samuel Taylor Coleridge, whose poetry attests to religious experience, and who, as a philosopher of considerable acuity, regarded the religious quest as "creeping towards the light" of God. A few decades later John Henry Newman argued that the voice of conscience is in truth the voice of God – so that, in attending to this voice, we are in communication with God. Such views may be termed "spiritual empiricism," and in recent times Richard Swinburne has offered the most cogent epistemological analysis.

Common challenge: other religions

When Augustus Toplady – first a supporter of Wesley, and then an ardent Puritan opponent – penned his famous hymn *Rock of Ages*, he had no doubt there could only be a single cleft in the rock offering shelter from the storms of sin, and that Christ stood at the entrance. Likewise, when Wesley preached to the artisans and peasants of Georgian England, Christianity was the only religion of which they had heard; so either they embraced the gospel, or they rejected religion altogether. And when Locke and Paley sought to prove the existence of a supreme intelligence, they assumed without question that this intelligence was identical with the God of the Bible.

But in the 19th century, as the British empire spread eastwards and southwards across the globe, and as explorers brought back tales from the remotest lands, the people of Britain became conscious of other religious beliefs and practices. And to their surprise they discovered that many of these beliefs were akin to those of Christianity, in both its Evangelical and Incarnational forms. Thus Islam is strongly Evangelical, asserting that Allah – who seems the same as the Christian God – has made a final and complete revelation of himself, which is contained in a book; and Muslims, like Christians, are charged by Allah with persuading as many people as possible to accept this revelation and live in accordance with it. The difference, of course, is that the book is the Koran, not the Bible. Hinduism, at least in some of its many forms, is strongly Incarnational, teaching that all existence embodies Atman, the universal divine spirit – which is identical with Brahman, the transcendent creator.

Moreover, there are many explicit connections between Christianity and other religions. The Koran acknowledges Jesus Christ as a prophet whose teachings came from Allah; and it incorporates several stories of the life of Christ – although they are sometimes at odds with the biblical narratives. Also medieval Christian theology adopted many ideas from Islam; and there were vigorous debates in Christian Europe about the ideas of the Muslim philosopher Averroes. Hinduism too may have absorbed Christian insights in ancient times when Christians from Syria settled on India's southwest coast. And contact with British Christians in the imperial period stimulated a reformation within Hinduism, producing several remarkable thinkers and activists, including Mahatma Gandhi.

Far from diminishing with the collapse of empire, awareness of the plurality of religions has continued to grow; and so has awareness of their similarity and links with Christianity. Indeed, the combination of the mass media, immigration between continents, and long-distance air travel has relegated Christianity in most people's eyes to one religion amongst many. No one now doubts that other religions can produce people – like Gandhi – of the same spiritual and moral stature as the Christian saints. And no one now imagines that Christianity has a monopoly of those spiritual gifts that Christians – especially Evangelicals – associate with conversion and commitment to Christ. They have seen television pictures of spiritual healers and prophets, and of people speaking and singing in tongues, from every corner of the world; and they have read of people in every religion having remarkable spiritual experiences, such as sensations of inner warmth.

For those outside the Christian fold there are now two popular views of the relationship between the different religions of the world. The first acknowledges that every religion is distinct, with its own particular ideas, but regards them as all teaching the same underlying truth. Thus in effect each religion has its own separate cleft in the rock of ages. The second sees all the religions as essentially the same, so that the ideas of one can be readily equated with the ideas of another, and they differ only in their outward forms – their rituals and symbols. Thus there is one huge cleft in the rock, with many paths leading to it. Those within the Christian fold reject both these views; but Evangelicals and Incarnationals reject them for entirely different reasons, and respond to other religions in entirely opposite ways.

Evangelicalism unambiguously asserts that there is still only one cleft in the rock, and that there is a single path leading to it. While other religions may share some of Christianity's ideas, salvation from sin is through Christ alone. For Puritans like Toplady Christ compels some to enter and some to stay out of the cleft, while for post-Wesley Evangelicals Christ beckons everyone that passes – and the cleft can expand to accommodate all who accept his invitation. Nonetheless it remains highly exclusive, and in some Evangelical eyes it even excludes Incarnationals, since, by failing to accept the Bible as the sole foundation for belief, they are not properly Christian.

Incarnationalism by contrast denies there are any clefts at all, and we should refuse to follow any path that leads us away from normal life. Our religious task is to discern divinity within ourselves and in the world around us. And we should expect religions across the world to help and encourage us in this discernment. Some religions may be better than others in this, and it is possible that some religions will have become so distorted and corrupt that they may actually blind people. Nonetheless Incarnational theology suggests most religions are likely to offer insights from which Christians can benefit, and that a few may be equal to Christianity in spiritual wisdom.

Despite the contrast between these two attitudes to religious plurality, they both raise awkward questions that are the mirror image of each other. For Evangelicals their wholesale rejection of other religions is difficult to square with their understanding of Christian conversion. If Hindus and Muslims, Buddhists and Taoists – and also, perhaps, the adherents of many tribal religions – can attain great holiness, if they can find that their hearts are strangely warmed, and if some can even speak in tongues, then how do these same spiritual gifts amongst Evangelical Christians confirm the unique truth of their own beliefs? And if they do not confirm it, why should anyone choose to embrace the gospel, rather than the message of Krishna, Muhammad, the Buddha or Lao Tzu? Thus the Puritans' anxieties about Wesley's denial of predestination and his doctrine of free choice return with a vengeance.

For Incarnationals their willingness to affirm the value of any and every religion is difficult to square with their own commitment to Christianity. If every religion is potentially valid, why not seek insight and inspiration from them all, as need and opportunity arises? For the first time in history all the major spiritual writings of the world, and many of the minor ones, have been translated into a single language, namely English; and the Anglican Church is peculiarly privileged in having English as its primary language. So would it not be rational for Incarnational Anglicans to dip freely into the religious treasure chest, and thence abandon the specifically Christian nature of their faith?

These questions are fundamentally epistemological in character. Those confronting Evangelical Christianity arise from its pragmatism – its linking of the truth of religious doctrines with the consequences of holding them. Those confronting Incarnationalism arise from its empiricism – its basing of religious belief on the nature of the human psyche. Yet in their search for answers Evangelicals and Incarnationals alike must delve more deeply into the relationship between the Bible and human experience. Evangelicals must explore afresh which particular aspects of human experience affirm the uniqueness of the biblical revelation; while Incarnationals have to show why the Bible should have a special and privileged place in enabling them to experience existence as divine. This suggests that if Evangelical and Incarnational Anglicans are serious about finding answers, they would do well to remain in close contact with one another. And in reality they have no choice but to be serious, since the entire credibility of their respective convictions are at stake.

CHAPTER 3:

MORALITY

Evangelical morality: frugality and fidelity

In his dialogue *Euthyphro* Plato quotes Socrates as asking:
"Is holiness holy because the gods approve it, or do they
approve it because it is holy?" After Christian monotheism
replaced Greek polytheism, this famous question came to
be re-formulated: "Is a right action right because God
commands it; or does God command a right action
because it is right?" The Evangelical reply is that an action
is right because God commands it – and an action is wrong
because God forbids it. Moreover, while the people of
Socrates' time had no reliable access to the divine will,
today we have the Bible. Hence we should seek moral
guidance from the Bible, and follow it unquestioningly.

Contrary to the strictures of many opposed to this view
(including Richard Hooker), Evangelicals have never
thought that the Bible provides a crude moral code; they

have always acknowledged a central role for biblical
scholars in interpreting the true meaning of biblical texts.
And, while they believe that the moral principles of the
Bible are inviolable, they have recognized that the
application of these principles may vary according to
circumstances. Thus in Calvin's time the issue of usury –
charging interest on loans – was as controversial as
homosexuality is today, and Calvin acknowledged that the
Bible forbade it. But he argued that the reason for this
prohibition was that, in biblical times, people only
borrowed money to alleviate poverty, so that the usurer
was taking advantage of their misfortune. By the 16th
century, however, money was being lent and borrowed to
finance trade and industry; so it was fair that the lender
should share the profits. Hence Calvin allowed interest to
be charged, but fixed a maximum rate.

According to the strict Calvinist doctrine of
predestination, the person chosen by God for salvation will
automatically obey God's moral laws – once he or she has
received the correct interpretation. Indeed, for Calvin
moral obedience to God is a visible sign of divine election.
And just as the inner spiritual consequences of being
Christian are irrelevant to the truth of the Bible, so the
outer consequences of obedience are irrelevant to the
rightness of biblical ethics. It was paradoxical, then, that
the consequences of following Calvin's moral guidance
proved so benign – as the sociologist Max Weber famously
argued. In addition to permitting usury, Calvin also
advocated frugality and thrift. Hence Calvinist investors
ploughed most of their profits back into investment,
growing hugely rich; and this in turn enabled the capitalist

system to develop and expand, bringing further enrichment.

To the Wesleyan Evangelical, by contrast, the consequences of biblical morality are highly relevant, proving that the Bible is right as well as true. Wesley himself never argued that obeying the Bible made you rich. In fact, he himself gave away to the poor any material gifts that he received, and he urged his wealthier followers also to be generous. But an hour or two watching religious TV channels in the USA demonstrates that many spiritual descendents of Wesley are only too happy to link Christian obedience with prosperity, as well as with various other worldly blessings such as good health. This, of course, raises the question of why faithful Christians sometimes suffer poverty and poor health, while wicked people often thrive. But even the Psalmist was vexed by this conundrum, as were Job and his comforters; so if Judaism and Christianity have grappled with it for so long, it can hardly be fatal to faith.

When it came to sex, Calvin largely adopted Augustine's view that sexual activity is intrinsically sinful, and is the means by which sin has been passed from one generation to another since Adam and Eve's original disobedience. Thus, as Augustine taught, Christians should only engage in sexual activity with the specific intention of procreation, and should take as little pleasure in it as possible. John Wesley, who was himself unhappily married, seems to have taken a similarly negative attitude; and, while Evangelicals after Wesley often extolled the blessings of happy marriage, their image of domestic bliss was sternly unromantic. However, during the 20th century Evangelical

Anglicanism gradually softened, and today many Evangelicals speak of sexual pleasure as a divine gift. Indeed, to my knowledge no Evangelical Anglican has objected to the change in the way in which the marriage service refers to sex. Cranmer's Prayer Book declared that God's second object in ordaining marriage was "a remedy against sin, and to avoid fornication." Modern Anglican prayer books across the world use some variant of the words in the Church of England's Alternative Service Book, published in 1980: marriage "is given that with delight and tenderness [husband and wife] may know each other in love, and through the joy of their bodily union may strengthen the union of their hearts and lives."

Undoubtedly the shift in Evangelical attitudes to sexual pleasure has been influenced by changes in secular culture. But secular culture has gone far further than Evangelicals are willing to follow. It is now commonplace in most western countries for a man and woman to live together and raise children without getting married; and this incurs little or no moral opprobrium in society at large. And young people typically expect to have several sexual partners before settling down into a stable relationship – although there remains a strong moral conviction that sexual partnerships should be consecutive rather than concurrent. Such behavior is reflected and enforced by the ubiquity of explicit sex on television and in films, and by the erotic imagery habitually used by advertisers. In the face of this sexual hurricane Evangelicals stand remarkably firm. They repeat at every opportunity that God wants sexual relations to be confined to marriage; so single people should abstain from sex, and those in unmarried partnerships should either marry or split.

There is, however, one important respect in which Evangelicals often compromise with secularity. The New Testament could hardly be clearer that marriage should be a lifelong commitment, and this has traditionally been taken to imply that even if a husband and wife separate they remain married – so neither can enter a new marriage while the spouse survives. Until one or two generations ago this prohibition on divorce and remarriage was seldom questioned in Evangelical circles, mainly because divorce amongst Evangelicals was so rare. But the current epidemic of divorce has infected Evangelicals along with almost every other group in society, and in most Evangelical Anglican congregations there are now couples who are married according to civil law but living in sin according to the old interpretation of biblical law. This situation appears to be accepted with little more than sighs of regret. And if Evangelicals are questioned about it, they generally reply that second marriages frequently bring great emotional blessings to those involved, and hence must be incurring divine approval. They also point to the biblical teaching on God's limitless capacity for forgiveness, asserting that he has forgiven whatever sins may have caused the first marriage to collapse.

This Evangelical response to second marriage neatly illustrates the philosophical status of Evangelical morality. It is based on divine commands, conveyed to humanity through the Bible. In its Puritan form these commands require no further justification or explanation, so that from a human viewpoint they are entirely arbitrary. But in its post-Wesley form they need to be confirmed by positive practical experience – just as the basic truth of the Bible needs confirmation through positive spiritual experiences. Within the sexual sphere Evangelicals have always been able to point to the happiness that a loving, faithful marriage can bring, using this to demonstrate the value of confining sex to marriage. But in the case of remarriage after divorce Evangelicals try to re-interpret the Bible in the light of experience. And most modern Evangelical couples manifestly re-interpret Paul's teaching on the obedience that a wife owes her husband, ordering their relationship to suit their respective personalities. So just as Evangelical theology is epistemologically pragmatic, so Evangelical morality is ethically pragmatic.

Incarnational morality: harmony and happiness

When John Locke turned his empirical eye towards human beings, it was clear to him that we are part of the natural order. Hence, like every other species, we are subject to natural laws that have been ordained by God; and, if we live in accordance with these laws, we are fulfilling God's purpose. However, we are different from other species in two crucial respects: first, we possess the faculty of reason, which enables us to reflect on our nature; and secondly, we have free will. Morality, therefore, consists in using our reason to determine the natural laws that apply to us, and in choosing to obey those laws. As he summarized his view: "Moral good and evil is only the conformity or disagreement of our voluntary actions to some law, whereby good or evil is drawn on us, from the will and power of the law-maker." Hence God's will is "the true ground of morality."

Locke's line of argument dominated moral thought amongst Incarnational Anglicans right up to the early decades of the 20th century. But Locke was far from original in this respect. In fact, he was following the moral philosophy of the great medieval theologian Thomas Aquinas. Aquinas in turn was influenced by the metaphysics of the Greek philosopher Aristotle (whose works, incidentally, had newly become available to the Christian world via Muslim scholars in Spain). Thus many Anglican moral thinkers referred directly back to Aquinas. They were encouraged in this by the Roman Catholic Church, which also based (and still bases) its moral teaching on Aquinas's ideas. According to Aquinas, we should apply the cool light of reason to every aspect of human nature and human relationships, and discern its divine purpose; we should then frame moral principles that enable us to fulfill that purpose.

Within the economic sphere Thomas Aquinas – following Aristotle – believed that the moral principle applying to all transactions is reciprocity: both sides in a transaction should enjoy equal gains. Thus when individuals sell the goods that they have made, they should charge a "just price" that gives them a proper reward for their labor. They should also be honest about their goods' defects as well as virtues, so that potential purchasers can assess the value of the goods to them. On the issue of usury, Aquinas argued that the principle of reciprocity forbids it, since people holding money incur no cost in lending it to others; so rich people should be willing to lend freely to the poor.

But just as Calvin found a means of re-interpreting the Bible in usury's favor, so, somewhat later, both Catholic and

Anglican natural law moralists applied similar ingenuity to the principle of reciprocity. Far from incurring no cost in lending money to others, individuals lose the opportunity of investing that money in their own enterprises. Thus people should charge the rate of interest that reflects the productivity of capital – which is the just price of money. Indeed, Locke himself observed that the forces of supply and demand generally lead to justice, in the markets for goods and for money alike.

On sexual matters natural law morality is far clearer, implying a principle whose practical application leaves little room for argument. The divine purpose of our sexual organs, so Thomas Aquinas asserted, is reproduction, therefore people should only engage in sexual activity with the intention of conceiving a child. This principle manifestly forbids masturbation and contraception, and also sexual intercourse after the female menopause. In addition it condemns pleasure as a motive for intercourse, even if conception is the potential consequence. Aquinas enunciated a further principle relating to the institution of marriage, that God created this institution primarily for the purpose of raising children. When the marital and sexual principles are combined, the conclusion is that sex should be confined to marriage.

Thus in both the economic and the sexual spheres – the two spheres on which Christian morality has most closely focused – Evangelicals and Incarnationals arrived at broadly the same rules. So, although their ways of reaching these rules were quite different, they saw no need to quarrel. But with the rise of Darwinism, and the consequent collapse of Locke's natural theology,

Incarnational Anglicans gradually abandoned natural law morality. For several decades they struggled to develop an alternative form of moral reasoning. Their efforts were somewhat haphazard and confused, as demonstrated by most of the reports on moral matters produced by the Church of England hierarchy during the second half of the 20th century. Nonetheless the "mystical" form of Incarnational theology – that of Coleridge, Maurice, Temple and their ilk – has clear moral implications, and these now seem to inform much of the moral debate within Incarnational circles.

The morality of mystical Incarnationalism is essentially about becoming Christ-like, and thence striving to "love your neighbor as yourself" – which may, in terms of moral philosophy, be regarded as the Christian definition of virtue. Christian virtue is typically then taken to imply two complementary ethical principles. First, individual human beings should seek to live in harmony with other human beings – and arguably in harmony with all living beings. Secondly, individuals should seek to live in harmony with themselves, fulfilling their own natures. The challenge of practical morality, therefore, is to reconcile these two principles – to find ways in which individual men and women can fulfill themselves, while simultaneously respecting the needs both of other people and of other species.

Within the economic sphere this challenge is manifestly both urgent and huge. Our economic activities are having dire effects not only on many of the other species with whom we share the planet, but also on one another, with much of humanity suffering chronic and inescapable poverty. The global nature of these problems illustrates an important facet of Incarnational morality: that satisfying its first principle generally requires collective, as well as individual, moral action. Thus individually we may try to be less polluting and wasteful, and we may give generously to international charities. But even if everyone acted in these ways, the aggregate of individual efforts would still not solve the problems. The solution also requires changes in the social and political framework of human behavior.

Within the sexual sphere, the problems mainly lie in satisfying the second principle, that of living in accordance with our own natures. This is partly because sexuality infuses almost every aspect of the human psyche; so sexual fulfillment can only be attained in the context of human fulfillment as a whole. It is also because our sexual needs and aspirations often conflict with one another. To take an obvious example, an individual may simultaneously want a faithful relationship with one partner, and also want sexual partnerships with various other people. A further problem is that sexuality changes greatly through the course of life, so sexual fulfillment for the elderly is quite different from that for the young.

The psychological complexity of human sexuality makes Incarnational Anglicans reluctant to lay down strict moral rules. Most Incarnationals continue to believe that a loving monogamous relationship, which both partners regard as permanent, is highly desirable. But they also recognize that monogamous relationships that were once loving can become mutually destructive and are best dissolved, and that for some people monogamy is never good. More controversially, some Incarnational Anglicans are open to the possibility that, within certain cultural contexts, various forms of polygamy may be right. Few, if any, Incarnationals maintain the old antipathy to contraception, and all accept mutual pleasure as a motive for sexual activity. Many, however, feel uncertain about the morality of erotic imagery and pornography, sensing that a line needs to be drawn but not knowing where to draw it. And, considering how positive both Jesus and Paul were about it, there is also a surprising degree of uncertainty about celibacy, with some regarding it as a valid sexual option, while others fear that is may be psychologically unhealthy.

Yet, regardless of the difficulties of applying the principles of Incarnationalism to specific moral issues, Incarnationals are united in their answer to Socrates' question, which is the exact opposite to the Evangelicals answer: for Incarnational Anglicans God commands right actions because they are right.

Common challenge: homosexual love

If Evangelical Anglicanism has achieved a degree of recognition by the general public across the globe, it is because of its firm and unrelenting opposition to homosexual relationships. Some Evangelicals understandably complain at this negative image, since their primary message – eternal joy through union with Christ – is positive. Yet this joy comes at a price, which includes, for those with homosexual orientation, suppressing sexual desire. And many Evangelicals have come to regard this issue as a test of faith: if an individual has accepted the Bible as the unique and complete divine revelation, then he or she will also accept homosexuality as wrong – because the Bible says it is.

Yet until a century ago this test would have been completely useless, and even as recently as two or three decades ago it would have been largely invalid. Most Incarnational Anglicans, in common with most of the population, also regarded homosexuality as wrong, on the grounds that it is unnatural. On this single issue Incarnational Anglicans continued to cling – without necessarily realizing it – to natural law morality, believing that the sexual organs were designed for heterosexual intercourse. Admittedly by the 1960s and 70s the majority of Incarnationals had decided that mutual pleasure was a legitimate motive for heterosexual intercourse, and so had dropped their previous opposition to artificial contraception. But they still felt repelled by the idea of homosexual intercourse, which seemed contrary to God's plan for the world.

In the past generation Incarnational Anglicans have almost unanimously reversed their opinion. In the first place they have finally and belatedly absorbed the moral implication of Darwinism – that nature has no moral purpose. This is mainly because several popular science writers have drawn out this implication with great verve and eloquence, and their ideas have percolated down to the press and television. More importantly, the scientific understanding of homosexuality has changed. Although by the 1960s the idea of homosexuality as a deliberate choice was discredited, many psychologists held to a Freudian view of homosexuality as a mental disorder, in which the individual's sexuality had become trapped in an adolescent "phase." It was widely believed that the cause was some imbalance in the parents' relationship, such as the mother being unduly dominant. But the trouble with this analysis was that there was almost no evidence for it, and today very few psychologists continue to give it credence. Instead, homosexuality is widely assumed to originate with some kind of genetic predisposition, and hence is as natural as heterosexuality. And although the idea of a "gay gene," which enjoyed much publicity a few years ago, has also been largely abandoned, evolutionary psychologists have formed various theories as to why homosexuality may actually be adaptive – so long as homosexuals form only a small proportion of the population. Within the context of Incarnational theology and morality, the conclusion is unavoidable: that homosexual intercourse is morally equivalent to heterosexual intercourse.

Thus Evangelicals and Incarnationals are now wholly opposed on this issue. And this mutual opposition is made all the more stark by the way in which Incarnational Anglicans treat the biblical teaching. In a cogent analysis of Paul's condemnation of homosexual relations, Jeffrey John (writing in *The Way Forward*) declares Paul to be "wrong." According to John, Paul did not recognize homosexuality as an "exclusive and predominant inclination," but instead believed "that homosexual acts are committed by naturally heterosexual people" who "willfully choose their unnatural perversion." To Evangelicals, of course, Paul's writings cannot be wrong, since, by virtue of appearing in the Bible, we know that they are divinely inspired. Hence Jeffrey John is wrong.

Yet both Evangelical and Incarnational lines of reasoning are each open to serious challenge, even on their own terms. As with morality in general, these challenges are mirror images of one another.

The challenge to Evangelical reasoning is most obvious, and has been made repeatedly in the present debate: if a genetic basis for homosexuality could be proved beyond doubt, then condemning homosexual relations would effectively treat homosexuality as a vocation to celibacy – and this seems to have no biblical basis. In fact, the challenge can be reframed in a way that is even more problematic. Since Evangelicals (in their post-Wesley form) believe that the consequences of biblical morality are benign, they need to show that homosexuals can be healed of their condition, and then enter satisfactory marriages. And, not surprisingly, Evangelical Anglicans are eager to relate stories of this happening. Yet there are also many stories of Evangelical homosexuals failing to change their orientation – or, worse still, imagining that they had changed it, and then entering disastrous marriages. At best Evangelicals must admit that the evidence is mixed.

Incarnationals, on the other hand, cannot ignore the Bible. Biblical scholars in the Incarnational mould, such as Christopher Rowland, argue that the Bible itself demands a critical approach. According to Rowland, Paul "pioneered an approach to the Bible ... [in which] we should not concentrate on the letter of the text, but try to get at the underlying point." He cites Paul's dictum that "the letter kills, but the Spirit gives life" (*The Guardian*, October 4th, 2003). So, according to this view, Jeffrey John shows no disrespect to the Bible in saying that Paul was mistaken on the facts of homosexuality. Yet Incarnationals must also show how the Spirit, speaking through the Bible, sheds light on these facts. One possibility is that the biblical teaching on heterosexual marriage should also apply to gay and lesbian partnerships – so all such partnerships should be sexually exclusive, be regarded as lifelong, and involve a formal religious commitment. Unfortunately gay and lesbian Anglicans are divided on this, with many saying that love between homosexuals is profoundly different from heterosexual love, and hence cannot be subject to the same moral discipline.

As with theology, so with morality, the problem for Evangelicals and Incarnationals alike is to relate the Bible with experience. And it is not inconceivable that over the coming decades the Evangelical and Incarnational views of homosexuality will gradually converge – especially if they remain in ecclesiastical proximity under the Anglican umbrella. Rowan Williams (in *The Way Forward*) suggests that the Bible's teaching on homosexuality could be subject to the same creative re-interpretation as its strictures on usury. At present Evangelicals appear utterly closed to such a project, but the weight of scientific and medical evidence against them may grow so great that they have little choice. Incarnationals for their part need to develop a homosexual morality that is consistent with biblical ethical principles, and the central biblical principle in this regard is surely Christ's dictum about two people becoming "one flesh."

CHAPTER 4:

ECCLESIOLOGY

Evangelical ecclesiology: stealing the devil's tunes

To the Puritans, the church – the true church – is the aggregate of people whom God has chosen for salvation. And these people should attend actual churches week by week in order to hear the Bible correctly expounded. So there need to be ministers well-versed in biblical theology who are able to preach with clarity and conviction. Christians must also praise God, expressing gratitude to him for saving them, and happily the Bible provides suitable words in the form of the psalms. So the psalms should be set to music – the God-given medium for praise – and Christians should join in singing them. As for mission, the only evangelistic obligation is to welcome those who hear God's call.

As Augustine had taught, the visible church – the membership of actual churches where sermons are preached and psalms sung – is not identical with the true church, since people not chosen by God often participate in church life for all kinds of worldly motives. Nonetheless it is important that actual churches should function as if their membership was confined to the saved, and not allow worldly concerns to corrupt them. Hence the Puritans of Elizabethan and Jacobean England strove hard to reform the Church of England in accordance with their ideals. Puritan scholars were prominent in the universities, nurturing future ministers on the pure milk of Calvinist doctrine, and Puritan patrons appointed Puritan clergy to their parishes. Puritan poets also rewrote the psalms in the form of ballads – the so-called "metrical psalms" – and set them to simple melodies.

John Wesley had no objections to the principles of Puritan worship: he too valued long sermons conveying biblical truth, and he liked to hear Christians singing God's praise. But he objected to Puritan practice. Sermons in Puritan churches were dry and too scholarly for popular consumption, and the psalm tunes were now a century and a half old. Wesley also believed that basing all hymns directly on the Bible denied the power of God's Spirit to put fresh words into the poet's pen. So Wesley himself set a new standard of preaching, using metaphors, aphorisms and illustrations that made the gospel accessible to even the humblest laborer. And his brother Charles transformed Christian hymnody by stealing the devil's tunes. He took songs that he heard in taverns and at fairs, and composed new words that were simultaneously profound and vivid.

In one respect, however, Wesley's ecclesiology was entirely different from that of the Puritans: for him evangelism is the primary and the ultimate goal of the church. Those already saved by God must deploy all their ingenuity and imagination, and devote all their available time and strength, to persuading others to be saved. Thus the sermons preached and the hymns sung at Christian worship should not only be for the benefit of existing members of the church, but should also be attractive to outsiders, drawing them in. And Christian preachers and musicians should go out to factories and farms, mines and mills. For Wesley there was no contradiction between ministering to those who have already embraced Christ, and reaching out to those in need of Christ, since a congregation vibrant with Christ's love will want to share it with others. Thus the mark of a congregation's love is its missionary zeal, and its fruit is growth in the congregation's size.

By the early 19th century, although many of Wesley's own followers had left the Anglican fold, the Evangelical revival pioneered by Wesley had reached a large number of Anglican churches that had formerly been Puritan; and many of these churches had installed galleries to provide additional seating. But a century and a half later Anglican Evangelicalism had grown as stale and dull as Puritanism had become in Wesley's time – and the galleries were empty and rotting. So when in 1967 the first National Evangelical Anglican Congress was held at Keele, in the English midlands, many Evangelicals were wondering whether they had any future within Anglicanism. Indeed, photographs of the gathering show row upon row of frowning clerics, all in black suits, looking like a convention of funeral directors. Yet John Stott, one of the most articulate speakers that Anglican Evangelicalism has ever produced, persuaded his comrades that the Church of England remained a worthy vessel from which to fish for souls; and he urged them to strive for promotion within the hierarchy of the Church, in order to make it an even better vessel.

In the three and a half decades since Stott's plea, Evangelical Anglicanism – in England and in almost every other province – has transformed itself. In the first place it has revitalized its clergy training, so that its theological colleges, once bywords for spiritual dreariness and intellectual sterility, have become vibrant and innovative, producing men and women of remarkably high caliber. As a result Evangelical preaching has re-discovered its Wesleyan vitality. At the same time a new generation of Evangelical hymn-writers have been composing lively and memorable melodies – although their words rarely match Charles Wesley's poetic genius. Modern Evangelicals have also gone far further than John Wesley would have approved in abandoning liturgical forms, and they are constantly inventing new styles of worship. And to accommodate continuous liturgical revolution they have ripped out the fixed pews that their Puritan forbears loved so much, and replaced them with chairs (upholstered, if the church is rich enough) that can be moved about at will. In fact, there is little in Evangelical worship at the start of the 21st century that the Keele delegates would recognize.

Until Keele most Evangelicals within the Church of England had been contemptuous of ecclesiastical preferment. Through the 16th and 17th centuries the majority of Puritans actually wanted to get rid of bishops and archbishops, regarding them as a financial and spiritual burden. But they were bitterly opposed by monarchs and aristocrats, who saw the ecclesiastical hierarchy as reflecting, and thence legitimizing, the secular hierarchical order – in King James's famous phrase, "No bishops, no king." Wesley too had little time for bishops, and the ultimate cause of Methodism's split with Anglicanism was Wesley usurping episcopal powers, ordaining men whom the bishops had rejected. But John Stott shrewdly recognized that, if Evangelicals formed a substantial presence on the episcopal bench, they could ensure that young people of Evangelical allegiance would become rectors and vicars. And within England, and through much of the Anglican Church, this policy has proved triumphantly successful.

Although Evangelicals today rarely refer to the old Puritan distinction between the visible and the true church, it informs Evangelical attitudes to ecumenism. They see little point in trying to merge different denominations into a single larger body, since such arrangements relate only to the visible church. They fear that the effort expended in achieving such unity will divert Christians from the task of reaching out to those who belong to no denomination. Yet they are willing to enter into ecclesiastical alliances if the participants can give one another practical help and encouragement – and thence serve the true church. So they happily belong to such bodies as the Evangelical Alliance and the Scripture Union, and also support various missionary societies.

Incarnational ecclesiology: in all things

While Evangelical ecclesiology draws a firm – albeit invisible – boundary around the true church, Incarnational ecclesiology draws no boundaries at all. Since all people participate in divinity, there can be no sharp distinction between Christian and non-Christian, and since all social relations are divine relations, there can be no sharp distinction between church and society. Thus the mission of the church is not to make all people Christian, but to enable all people to live in accordance with divinity, as Christ did. And the members of the church are those who want both to benefit personally from its mission, and to support its mission for the benefit of others.

If this Incarnational mission, in its Anglican form, could be exemplified in the life and work of a single individual, that person would be George Herbert who died in 1633. His most famous prose work, normally given the title *The Country Parson*, describes his aspirations as a priest. His biography, written a few decades after his death by Izaak Walton, suggests that he largely fulfilled those aspirations. After a youth devoted to worldly pleasures and classical scholarship, he suffered what appears to have been a mental breakdown, emerging from it with a robust Christian faith. His tortuous spiritual path to Christ is revealed in his astonishing poetry. He was initially rector of a village west of Cambridge called Leighton Bromswold, and in 1630 he settled with his new wife at Bemerton, close to Salisbury. His ministry at Bemerton is the core of Walton's biography and the focus of *The Country Parson*, while the church at Leighton Bromswold, which he rebuilt and re-ordered according to his ecclesiological vision, is his memorial.

The most striking feature of Leighton Bromswold church is what appear to be two pulpits on either side of the chancel arch. The left pulpit is for preaching, and the one on the right is where the priest leads prayers. Herbert's understanding of prayer – and thence his theology and morality – is encapsulated in the opening verse of his most famous poem, *The Elixir*:

> *Teach me, my God and King,*
> *In all things thee to see,*
> *And what I do in any thing,*
> *To do it as for thee.*

His view of sermons is contained in *The Country Parson*: "He procures attention by all possible art … Sometimes he tells them stories, and sayings of others … but the character of his sermon is holiness." Thus through prayer we apprehend divinity in daily life, and through preaching we learn to conduct daily life in harmony with divinity.

According to Walton, George Herbert and his wife used to walk together from their rectory to the church for Morning and Evening Prayer, and rang the bell at the start of each service to remind the parishioners of God's presence at the heart of their community. And for Herbert the church building itself is a kind of sacrament in stone. So the parson should ensure that "all things be in good repair, as walls plastered, windows glazed, seats whole, firm and uniform," and the church should "be swept, and kept clean without dust or cobwebs." He also regarded the regular annual festivals – the "folk religion" of the English countryside – as sacramental, providing people with symbols and rituals that touch their lives directly. Thus the parson should be "a lover of old customs, if they be good and harmless; and the rather, because country people are much addicted to them, so that to favor them therein is to win their hearts." His own particular favorite appears to have been Rogation, when the parson leads the people round the parish, asking "a blessing of God for the fruits of the field" and "justice in the preservation of bounds."

Perhaps the most telling indication of Herbert's ecclesiology was his view of the parson's pastoral ministry. The parson should visit on weekdays, not on Sundays, so "he shall find his flock most naturally as they are, wallowing in the midst of their affairs." His first concern is that they are "in a competent way earning their living," and if they lack any material necessities, he should use church funds to help them. But he should also satisfy himself that they do not "labor anxiously, when they overdo it, to the loss of their quiet and health." Then he should enquire whether any in the house are sick. In Herbert's view the parson should be well versed in medicine, and should grow medicinal herbs in his garden. So if he finds someone ill, he should go back to his rectory, prepare the appropriate potion or poultice, and then return to administer it. Finally he should also ask after their mental well-being; and even if he finds them "in a peaceable state," he still exhorts them "to be vigilant, and not to let go the reins as soon as the horse is easy."

If George Herbert had given advice to bishops as well as to parsons, he would no doubt have urged them to offer the same kind of pastoral care to the rich and powerful figures in society as parsons should to humbler folk. He also would have told them to treat their great cathedrals as sacraments of God's presence in society as a whole. Certainly this has been the view of the respective roles of bishops and cathedrals that most Incarnational Anglicans have held. As a result Incarnational clergy have tended to be more eager for preferment to the episcopate than Evangelicals. And clergy and laity alike have been eager to maintain the cathedrals inherited from medieval times, and, where necessary, create new cathedrals of comparable splendor.

It seems likely that Herbert turned his mind occasionally to the small but growing number of extreme Puritans who refused to belong to the Church of England, and he surely regarded them with charity and good will. Indeed, shortly before his mental breakdown he delivered a speech to the king and his court on the futility of war against other nations; so he must have regarded conflict within the nation with even greater horror. In the centuries after Herbert the record of Incarnational attitudes to other denominations is somewhat mixed. Locke, whose childhood had coincided with the bloodshed of the English Civil War, consistently argued the case for religious toleration, partly in order to maintain peace, and partly because no single Christian church has sole access to truth. But many bishops of Incarnational persuasion believed the ecclesiastical unity was essential for national unity, and right up until the early 19th century such bishops persecuted and victimized both Protestant dissenters and Roman Catholics.

In the 20th century these opposing views coalesced. On the one hand, no Incarnational continued to hope that the Church of England could enjoy a religious monopoly. On the other hand, almost all Incarnationals concluded that a degree of unity between different religious groups was both desirable in itself, and also an aid to social harmony. As a result Incarnationals became virtually unanimous in their support for Christian ecumenism. More surprisingly, many Incarnationals were quick to extend their ecumenical commitment to the other religions of the world. So when in 1893 the first so-called Parliament of Religions was held in Chicago, Incarnational Anglicanism was strongly represented. In subsequent inter-faith gatherings, both international and local, Incarnational Anglicans continued to play prominent roles. Herbert himself seems to have anticipated some kind of global ecumenism when he wrote: "God in all ages hath his servants to whom he hath revealed his truth; ... and that as one country doth not bear all things, so there may be commerce, so neither hath God opened, or will open, all to one, that there may be traffic in knowledge between the servants of God." And the most famous of all global ecumenicists, Mahatma Gandhi, had an Incarnational Anglican, C F Andrews, as one of his closest companions.

Common challenge: decline and expansion

When in the Victorian period the Church of England sent missionaries across the globe – to lands "unvisited, unblest" – church going was at its height in the home country. The proportion of the population attending Sunday worship had risen steeply from its slump on the 18th century, and was probably almost as high as it had been in George Herbert's time. And since the total population of England had grown hugely, the total number of bottoms on pews was far greater. Even more striking was the proportion of people who marked their journey through life with the rituals that the Church of England provided. At the time of Queen Victoria's death in 1901, two-thirds of babies were still being baptized in the Church's fonts, and a half of those went on to be confirmed; almost 85% were married at the Church's altars; and Church of England clergy conducted around 90% of funerals.

The Church of England retained its spiritual dominance right through to the middle years of the 20th century. As recently as the early 1960s, when John Lennon declared that the Beatles were bigger than Jesus Christ, the proportion of babies being baptized into the Church of England had dropped only to around 60%, and three-quarters of marriages were still being solemnized in parish churches. So England remained a genuinely Anglican nation, as it had been since King Henry VIII's quarrel with the pope.

But no more. By 1979 Sunday attendance at Church of England services (according to impressive research carried out by Peter Brierley and his team) had fallen to well below two million, representing around 5% of the nation's population. During the following decade it plummeted to a million and a quarter, and by 1998 it was below a million – almost halving in only two decades. Worse still, the drop in attendance was far greater amongst children and young people than amongst the middle-aged and elderly, suggesting that the decline will continue, and may even become steeper, in the years to come. Indeed, this was confirmed in the first two years of the new century, when church attendance fell by a further 8%. And there has been a corresponding rejection of the Church's rites of passage. Now less than one baby in seven is baptized, only about one teenager in 20 is confirmed (although adult confirmations have risen), and about one marriage in three is in church.

This decline has not, however, been evenly spread between the two parties within the Church. In fact, the entire decline has been in Incarnational churches, while attendance at churches designating themselves Evangelical has actually risen very slightly – by 2% during the 1990s. In addition to the transformation in their styles of worship, there are probably two further factors that have enabled Evangelicals to hold their own. The first is that they have concentrated their efforts on relatively few churches, so that each church has a large congregation. This not only adds to the vibrancy of the worship, but also offers greater opportunities for making friends – an important attraction in the "lonely crowd" of modern towns and cities. The second is that Evangelical Anglican churches appear to have drawn worshipers from independent Evangelical churches, whose congregations dropped by over a third during the 1990s. Indeed, I know personally several areas of England where the local Anglican Evangelical church has become so superior in its worship and ministry that other Evangelical churches have been virtually bled dry.

But while Evangelicals in the Church of England have responded with agility to current challenges, Incarnationals have been conspicuously flat-footed. Most Incarnational clergy have long ago abandoned George Herbert's practice of walking round the parish on weekdays and knocking on doors. While they struggle to maintain the old annual festivals, in many places it is only the Christmas carol service that still fills the church. Yet they are at a loss to know what else to do. Worse still, in rural areas they struggle to maintain the ancient church – Herbert's stone sacrament – in every community, and to hold regular services. But a tiny congregation of the old and infirm, their breath visible in the cold, damp atmosphere as they struggle through Victorian hymns, is hardly likely to attract a new generation. Thus they are caught in a vicious circle. And this is given an extra twist by the erosion of the Church's historic wealth, which used to finance clergy stipends; now the stipends must be raised from parishioners themselves. This extra financial pressure is undoubtedly a further reason for people staying away from church, which in turn puts even greater pressure on those who remain.

In 1999 George Carey, towards the end of his term as Archbishop of Canterbury, declared that the Church of England "is one generation away from extinction." Such a dire prognosis is undoubtedly justified in relation to its Incarnational party; and it can only be proved wrong if, as a matter of extreme urgency, Incarnationals find new ways of relating to English culture. Just as George Herbert recognized the spiritual value of England's traditional symbols and rituals, so modern Incarnationals should be creative – and courageous – in finding and developing symbols and rituals that both appeal to the contemporary imagination, and convey a sense of divinity. But Evangelical Anglicans also need creativity and courage. Although their congregations are not declining, nor are they significantly expanding; and the total number of Evangelicals in England is falling, suggesting that Evangelical Christianity as a whole is failing to connect with modern sensibilities. The fact is that Evangelical worship, although it has done much catching up, remains behind the times. Its new hymns are mainly a stylistic cross between Buddy Holly and Simon and Garfunkel; and its preaching owes too much to the techniques deployed by Billy Graham when Buddy Holly topped the charts.

The problems of the Church of England are repeated, although in less acute form, in the other provinces where the Church was founded mainly by English settlers – such as the United States and Canada, Australia and New Zealand. In many other provinces, by contrast, Anglicanism is expanding; and the greatest numerical success stories are in sub-Saharan Africa. Thus Nigeria is now the largest Anglican province, and taken together the African provinces probably now account for well over half the total Anglican membership. But Africa has long suffered from what missionaries used to call "nominalism." While large numbers profess to believe the Christian gospel, their belief has little or no effect on their lives. I have heard many an Anglican in Uganda and Sudan, the two African provinces I know best, actually say "I am an uncommitted Christian," or perhaps "an unconverted Christian," which signifies a social attachment to the Anglican Church combined with moral and spiritual indifference. This problem originates in part in the gulf between the form of Christianity which most African provinces espouse, and the traditional religion of Africa. If the studies by the early anthropologists are correct, the traditional religions were almost all Incarnational in character, stressing the divinity of nature, but the Anglican mission was mainly Evangelical, with the Church Missionary Society playing a leading role. Although the traditional religions now have few formal adherents, their vestigial influence remains strong. For most Africans the leap to Evangelical Christianity seems to be too great, or perhaps they are not convinced in their hearts that they should make it.

Although I hesitate to offer advice to churches in such different cultures from my own, I have long felt that Anglicanism in many African provinces would be healthier if it had a viable Incarnational party, providing a stepping-stone between traditional African religions and full-blown Evangelicalism. It might also create a form of Christianity that combines the teaching of Christ with all that is good in the traditional religions. And such thoughts also have resonance in England and the English settler provinces of Anglicanism. Many people who in adult life convert to Evangelicalism, becoming totally biblical in their faith, spent their early years in an Incarnational parish. Incarnational religion sowed the seeds of their Evangelical faith. Conversely, many of the current pillars of Incarnational parishes first adopted Christianity at Billy Graham crusades and at university missions led by the likes of David Watson.

Thus in situations of both decline and expansion Evangelical and Incarnational Anglicanism have much to gain from one another.

CHAPTER 5:

PROPOSALS FOR THE CHURCH OF ENGLAND

Concerning distinctions

There can be little doubt that the Church of England
contains substantial numbers of both Evangelicals and
Incarnationals; so there clearly needs to be parallel
episcopal oversight of the kind proposed in the first chapter.

It is tempting to conclude from Peter Brierley's statistics
that the two parties are at present roughly the same size –
although the Incarnational party is shrinking rapidly. But until
congregations actually decide for themselves to which party
they belong, any such estimates are highly speculative. When
faced with the direct question of whether they would be
willing to accept the ministry of a priest in a homosexual
partnership, many churchgoers would have to look very
deeply into their consciences, and the outcome is hard to

predict.

This moral struggle suggests that both individuals and congregations may change their minds as the years pass. Some people may come to regard their initial antipathy to homosexual priests as an irrational prejudice, and others may come to regard their initial willingness to accept homosexual priests as arising from weakness of faith or theological ignorance. And there is little point in the Evangelical and Incarnational parties remaining within the same ecclesiastical entity unless people can move freely between them. Significantly, the Episcopal Ministry Act of Synod 1993, which provides for special episcopal oversight for those opposed to the ordination of women as priests, has a specific clause (9[1]) allowing congregations to alter their view at any time.

If parallel episcopal oversight for Evangelical and Incarnational parishes – or, indeed, special oversight for parishes opposed to the ordination of women – had been introduced a few generations ago, it would have put an unfair burden on churchgoers who found themselves in a parish with different convictions from their own. But now most people in England have cars; and churchgoers with cars are generally happy to give lifts to those without. And as result of this mobility many people already attend a church outside their own parish. So if a church opts for episcopal oversight contrary to an individual's convictions, the individual will readily be able to move to a church with the other kind of episcopal oversight. Moreover, parallel episcopal oversight will give potential churchgoers a clear indication of the convictions of each congregation, making it easier for them to find a suitable church.

So the first proposal is:

Congregations should be both free to choose, and also free at any time to alter their choice, between Evangelical and Incarnational episcopal oversight.

Concerning law

When King Henry VIII broke with Rome, there was confusion and disagreement about the consequences for English church life of this radical step. So it was decided that in the short-term the fewest possible changes should be made to the laws governing the church, and that laws should only be revised when some kind of consensus had emerged. This policy was enshrined in the Submission of the Clergy Act 1533. This Act set up a commission to ponder legal matters at leisure; and its final section stated that in the meantime all ecclesiastical laws and customs "which are not contrariant or repugnant to the laws, statutes and customs of this realm" should continue in force. In other words, old ecclesiastical laws hindering progress could be deemed "contrariant and repugnant," and thence bent or quietly ignored – so long as good order was not threatened. In the event it took until 1603 for a new legal code governing the Church of England to be promulgated.

This legal caution and flexibility seems an admirable precedent for the present situation. Obviously some equivalent of the Episcopal Ministry Act is required to establish parallel episcopal oversight. But this will set in motion a period of ecclesiological creativity, in which

Evangelicals and Incarnationals work out the implications for church life of their particular ecclesiological principles. And clearly it will take time before these implications are sufficiently clear to be given legal expression.

However, it would be unwise to wait several decades before further changes in the law are considered, since good ecclesiastical laws provide a valuable framework for ministry and mission. Following the example of our Tudor ancestors some kind of commission should be appointed. But unlike the earlier commission, it should actively encourage people to reflect on which laws need amending. Then, as a common view emerges on any particular law, the commission should make recommendations.

Thus the second proposal is:

> *Apart from the legislation to establish parallel episcopal oversight, there should in the first instance be no changes in the law governing the Church of England. And where existing laws are infringed in such a manner as not to threaten good order, no action should be taken. A commission should be established to recommend further legal changes as and when their desirability becomes manifest.*

Concerning choice

The Episcopal Ministry Act of Synod 1993 authorized the appointment of provincial episcopal visitors (PEVs) – the so-called "flying bishops" – for parishes opposed to the ordination of woman as priests, and parishes wanting their oversight had to petition their diocesan bishop. There are two important legal principles in this arrangement relevant to the present situation. In the first place parishes cannot be put under any legal obligation to choose between alternative forms of episcopal oversight, so there needs to be a "default" position for parishes that do not indicate a preference. Secondly, the default position should be the *status quo*. Although the ordination of women as priests was an innovation, it had nonetheless been legally approved, making it the *status quo*. Hence it was quite logical that the default position was the oversight of bishops willing to ordain women.

In the present situation determining the *status quo* is more problematic. On the one hand, there is a long history of active homosexuals being ordained and engaging in parochial ministry; indeed, Rowan Williams appears to have ordained an active homosexual during his time as bishop of Monmouth. On the other hand, there has been the expectation that active homosexual priests are "discreet." When I was training for ordination in the late 1970s, a fellow trainee was thrown off the course not for being actively homosexual, but for being open about it. More importantly, any kind of sexual activity outside marriage is manifestly contrary to the customary moral discipline of the clergy. So the default position must be that parishes are not prepared to accept the ministry of a priest in a homosexual partnership.

Incarnationals may object that the default position is likely to become the norm. In the first place, many parishioners will simply prefer to avoid long, and potentially divisive, discussions amongst themselves. Secondly, they may fear that, if they express a willingness to have a priest in a homosexual partnership, then this is the only kind of priest that their bishop will offer them. However, Incarnationals would be wise to welcome the challenge of having to persuade parishes of their case, as this will sharpen their theology. And those parishes opting for Incarnationalism will be highly committed to it, and thence willing to develop new forms of Incarnational ministry and mission – potentially spearheading an Incarnational revival. Evangelicals by contrast already have a sharp theology, and have long been enjoying a revival.

There is a further advantage in making non-acceptance of priests in homosexual partnerships the default position: it will help the majority of Anglican provinces, who are currently strongly opposed to homosexual priests, to remain at peace with the mother province. Rightly or wrongly, most provinces would be profoundly offended if Incarnationalism became the *status quo* in England, but they would probably offer little objection to making special provision for Incarnationals. Conversely, those provinces with a substantial body of Incarnationals would feel that the mother province was maintaining her long history of being inclusive and comprehensive.

Thus the third proposal is:

> *Parishes should be given the opportunity to petition the diocesan bishop for oversight by a bishop who is willing to ordain and license priests in a homosexual partnership.*

Concerning bishops

The Suffragan Bishops Act 1534 declared that a suffragan

bishop is appointed by the diocesan bishop to assist him. Since a suffragan has full sacramental authority, he can perform any function that the diocesan bishop may wish to delegate, including the ordination of priests and deacons. Under the Dioceses Measure 1978 the role of suffragans was given a significant boost: the Measure allowed a "scheme" to be introduced dividing a diocese into "areas," and thence designating each suffragan an "area bishop" with virtually the same powers as a diocesan bishop. The PEVs instituted by the Episcopal Ministry Act of Synod 1993 are technically suffragan, but they function on a provincial rather than a diocesan basis, and, as the ecclesiastical lawyer Mark Hill has observed (in *Ecclesiastical Law*), are for all practical purposes equivalent to diocesan bishops.

Legislation similar to the Episcopal Ministry Act of Synod should be enacted authorizing the appointment of PEVs who are avowedly Incarnational, in the sense that they support the ministry of priests in homosexual partnerships. The legislation should also authorize parishes to petition their diocesan bishop for Incarnational episcopal oversight. In some cases one of the bishops in the diocese, diocesan or suffragan, will himself be Incarnational, and be willing to provide such oversight. But if not, the parish would be put under a PEV. It is impossible to foresee how many PEVs are likely to be required, so the legislation should not specify a number but simply allow the archbishops of Canterbury and York to appoint as many as they see fit.

Experience in the Episcopal Church of the USA suggests

that, where the diocesan bishop is Incarnational, strongly Evangelical parishes may not be willing to accept his oversight, and there are already some instances of this occurring in England. Obviously, where there is a suffragan bishop with Evangelical convictions, then such parishes can have his oversight. But if this is not the case, then it would seem wise in the short-term to make *ad hoc* arrangements, inviting an Evangelical bishop from a neighboring diocese, or a retired bishop in the area, to provide oversight. In the longer term at least one bishop in every diocese should be Evangelical, to the extent that he is avowedly opposed to homosexual partnerships. There is no need to legislate for this, but instead it can be achieved through informal understanding – similar to the understanding in the past that ensured that one of the English archbishops was "high" while the other was "low."It is quite possible that the number of Incarnational parishes will grow such that in certain dioceses a bishop can be fully employed providing oversight to them. In such cases it would seem wise to dispense with the ministry of a PEV, and instead ensure that one of the bishops of the diocese – diocesan or suffragan – is Incarnational. But again this can evolve through informal understanding.

Thus the fourth proposal is:

> *Legislation should be enacted, comparable with the Episcopal Ministry Act of Synod 1993, instituting provincial episcopal visitors for parishes that petition the diocesan bishop for oversight by a bishop willing to ordain and license priests in a homosexual partnership.*

Concerning parishes choosing

The Episcopal Ministry Act of Synod confers on the parochial church council (PCC) of a parish the duty of choosing whether to petition the bishop. This would also be sensible in the current circumstances. The alternative would be to put the matter to the entire electoral roll of the parish. But a decision such as this should involve discussion and debate, for which the PCC is the proper forum. Nonetheless it would be wise for PCC members to consult both other electoral roll members, and other parishioners who are not on the electoral roll.

But, contrary to the precedent of the Episcopal Ministry Act of Synod, it would be right to separate the clergy from the laity. Thus the incumbent of the parish, and any other clergy on the PCC, should absent themselves when the PCC is deciding whether to petition the bishop. The reason for this is that the implications of such a petition are quite different for clergy and laity, and so they have distinct, and potentially divergent, interests. For the laity the main practical implication is the sort of priest that they are likely to be offered as and when their present incumbent resigns. But for the clergy the choice of episcopal oversight is likely to have substantial consequences for their future careers and for the discipline to which they are subject – points explored below. Such differences of interests do not occur in relation to the ordination of women.

So the fifth proposal is:

> *A decision by a parish of whether to petition the diocesan bishop should be taken by the parochial church council, with the exclusion of any clergy members.*

Concerning priests choosing

On theological matters bishops in the Church of England have always had little choice but to allow a high degree of latitude amongst their priests. The Thirty-Nine Articles, the Church of England's doctrinal formulae that were finally agreed in 1571, avoid narrow definitions and were probably deliberately intended by their framers to allow a variety of interpretations. Besides, since 1865 clergy have been required only to teach nothing in contradiction to them, rather than positively to subscribe to them. But on moral matters bishops have generally been much firmer, and there have been at least three reasons for this. First, moral lapses are visible, whereas theological heresy is in the mind. Secondly, the English have always placed particular importance on family life, and have wanted clergy families to be exemplars. And thirdly, while Evangelicals and Incarnationals have disagreed over many things, they have until recently had a high degree of agreement on moral practice.

However, as we have seen, this agreement has now broken down, with homosexual partnerships being the major, though not the only, focus of dispute. Thus the moral discipline imposed by Incarnational bishops will be substantially different from that imposed by Evangelical bishops. Obviously Incarnational bishops will allow homosexual priests to have partners. Also, while there is no consensus amongst Incarnationals as to whether homosexual partnerships should be lifelong, Incarnational bishops will have to allow homosexual priests to change partners without disciplinary repercussions. And by extension Incarnational bishops are likely to condone divorce and remarriage amongst heterosexual priests in their charge.

So in choosing whether to seek Incarnational episcopal oversight, a priest is deciding which type of discipline he or she wishes to accept. And this in turn has important implications for the priest's career. It would manifestly be unreasonable and wrong to expect, or even ask, a parish to accept an Incarnational priest if the parish had not petitioned for Incarnational episcopal oversight – since the parishioners could properly expect the priest to be under Evangelical discipline. As a result Incarnational priests will only be able to have posts in Incarnational parishes.

In the short-run there is obviously a danger that some incumbents opt for Incarnational oversight, while their parishes do not; and there is also a danger (though it seems much less) of parishes opting for Incarnational oversight while their incumbents do not. If there is mutual trust between incumbent and parishioners, this should not present a problem. But in a few cases where trust is already lacking, then this could lead to pastoral breakdown. At present most situations of pastoral breakdown are sorted out discreetly, and this would surely occur here. But if discretion failed, the procedures laid out under The Incumbents (Vacation of Benefices) Measure 1977 could be invoked.

Thus the sixth proposal is:

> *The legislation should allow clergy, separately from the parishes in which they may currently be serving, to petition the diocesan bishop for oversight by a bishop who is willing to ordain and license priests in a homosexual partnership.*

Concerning church government

The government of the Church of England is a curious mixture of hierarchy and democracy. Bishops are appointed by the crown, and they in turn appoint archdeacons and rural deans. But the laity elects lay members of deanery synods, who in turn elect lay members of the diocesan synods and the General Synod. There are serious flaws in these arrangements, both in theory and in practice, but in the present situation the important question is whether the advent of provincial episcopal visitors for Incarnational parishes is likely to pose particular problems.

The appointment of PEVs in response to the ordination of women has had virtually no impact on church government as a whole, and in purely constitutional terms the new PEVs will be equally insignificant. Archdeacons and rural deans should have no difficulty in continuing to perform their legal functions, which are mainly of an administrative nature, and parishes under PEVs could continue to send representatives to their deanery synod. Obviously there would be a somewhat clearer demarcation of the parties within the Church of England, and this could lead to more factionalism within synods, especially the General Synod – which is the only level of synodical government with substantial power. But, by separating episcopal oversight, the members of each party will feel more secure in their pattern of church life, and hence may become less prone to look at issues purely in party terms.

The main danger is the one to which Stephen Sykes alludes in his foreword to *The Way Forward*. He refers to the disgust – which is quite distinct from disapproval – that some Evangelicals show towards homosexuals with partners, and also to the tendency of homosexuals to regard Evangelicals as bigots and "homophobes." People with such hostile attitudes may refuse to participate in the same ecclesiastical bodies as the objects of their hostility. If this became widespread then, as Stephen Sykes fears, there would *de facto* schism, and if it were prolonged, the schism would have to become *de jure*. But if it were confined to only a few people on either side then it could be safely ignored, with those refusing to participate merely being marked down as absent in the appropriate minutes. Stephen Sykes appeals for Christian charity on both sides, and again the greater security provided by separate episcopal oversight might soften people's hearts. Indeed, a strong argument for limited change now, in the form of parallel episcopates, is that it is likely to halt the momentum towards much greater change – total schism – in the future.

Keeping the present system of church government largely unaltered conforms, of course, to the general principle of minimizing immediate legal changes. However, the need for PEVs, arising from the theological and moral differences of the two main parties within the Church, suggests that the system may in fact be too tight and restrictive. My own hunch is that, if the Church of England had retained the much looser form of church government that existed until the 20th century, the present difficulties could have been handled and contained by informal means. And in general good ecclesiastical law allows very wide scope for diversity – for the Spirit to blow where it wills. So the legal commission recommended above should use the present difficulties as the stimulus for a wider review of the Church of England's constitutional arrangements.

Thus the seventh proposal is:

> *Following the appointment of PEVs there should in the short-term be no further changes in the system of church government. In the longer term the commission recommended in the second proposal should include within its remit a general review of church government, exploring whether it allows sufficient freedom to parishes.*

Concerning money

From the inception of the English parochial system in Anglo-Saxon times, parish churches enjoyed a high degree of financial autonomy. Money was raised within each parish by a variety of means, and it was then spent on the priest's stipend and the church building. Inevitably this led to inequalities between parishes. But from the early 18th century these were partly offset by a central fund, Queen Anne's Bounty, which augmented low stipends, and many priests topped up their stipends by other work, such as tutoring.

However, in the course of the 20th century the financing of ministry passed from parochial to diocesan control. Thus the diocese now levies a quota on each parish, assessed by some formula for ensuring that it is proportionate to the parish's ability to pay. The diocese then uses the quota income from all the parishes to pay clergy stipends. There are two obvious advantages of this: that the stipends of the clergy are equal, and that richer parishes subsidize poorer ones. But there are substantial disadvantages. First, while some parishes are poor because parishioners have low incomes, others are poor because parishioners are ungenerous, and there is no good reason why meanness should be subsidized. Secondly, and more importantly, by destroying the link between the money people contribute and the ministry they receive, the system eliminates any incentive for parishioners to develop their own voluntary ministry. On the contrary, the incentives work in the reverse direction: loyal parishioners must devote so much time and effort to raising money for the quota, that they have little opportunity to develop and exercise their spiritual gifts. It is small wonder that the initiatives in numerous dioceses to encourage voluntary ministry have borne so little fruit.

In my own view the centralization of finances has been a major cause of the decline in the Church of England over the past 30 years. As the historic resources of the Church have dwindled (partly, though not wholly, owing to mismanagement), the proportion of clergy stipends covered by quota income has risen, and is now approaching a hundred percent. Thus there has been mounting pressure on churchgoers to put more money into the collection, and to organize more and better fund-raising events. In addition to diverting effort from voluntary ministry, this has also in effect raised the price of churchgoing. While committed churchgoers have been willing to pay the price, many potential churchgoers have been deterred. And as congregations have fallen, so the pressure on remaining churchgoers has become even greater, causing congregations to fall further. Thus many parishes in the Church are caught in a vicious circle of failure.

One hugely benign consequence of parallel episcopates is that this system will become unworkable. The parishes with the largest incomes are mostly Evangelical; and they can hardly be expected to support Incarnational parishes. Indeed, when Jeffrey John was appointed to Reading, there were threats that Evangelical parishes might withhold their quota, driving the diocese towards bankruptcy. Thus at the very least there will have to be two separate diocesan funds into which quotas are paid. But since Incarnational oversight will be organized on a provincial, rather than diocesan, basis, this would be exceedingly complex to administer.

The obvious answer is to abandon the system altogether, and adopt a modern version of the decentralized system that served the Church of England well for over a millennium – and which remains the norm in most other Anglican provinces. Parishes would make their own ministerial arrangements within the laws and customs of the Church; and, in accordance with the law, they could only have the ministry of priests and deacons licensed or permitted by their bishop. Thus they could choose to have one or more full-time clergy, raising the money to pay for them. Or they could pay clergy as and when they need them – many priests (like myself) might have ministry as part of a "portfolio" of sources of income. And, of course, parishioners would have every incentive, spiritual and financial, to put their own spiritual gifts at the service of their parish. The old patronage system has, since the Pastoral Measure 1983, become so flexible that it could easily accommodate this decentralization. Indeed, in purely legal terms, it represents virtually no change from what already occurs in many parts of the country.

Under such an arrangement parishes would only be asked to pay a comparatively modest quota to cover the central costs of the Church – including the costs of their own bishop, ministerial training, and so on – not covered by the Church's historic resources. Dioceses could offer parishes (for a fee) a payroll service to cope with the administrative aspects of employing priests. Alternatively, parishes wanting this service could employ a private specialist. Various voluntary funds would doubtless develop through which richer parishes could support poorer ones – indeed, some still survive from earlier times – and some richer parishes could offer direct help. This form of support, given freely out of a generous spirit, may prove to be far greater than the support currently channeled through the quota, and it will certainly be used to better effect. And, of course, the subsidy to the Judean church, raised by Paul, provides an excellent biblical precedent – where, significantly, Paul refused to lay down any rules.

So the eighth proposal is:

> *Parishes should become financially autonomous. They should determine their own provision of ordained ministry, with the approval of their bishop and patrons, as the law requires. And richer parishes should be encouraged to support poorer ones. Parishes should be required to pay their share of central costs not covered by the Church's historic resources.*

Concerning selection and training

Obviously a candidate for the priesthood in a homosexual partnership would not be regarded as suitable by an Evangelical bishop, but might be approved by an Incarnational one. And an Evangelical bishop would look for somewhat different doctrinal convictions from those sought by his Incarnational counterpart. But the differences go beyond theology and moral practice, and extend to gifts and abilities. Evangelical ecclesiology requires that ordained ministers are eloquent and inspiring preachers, and can lead worship with flair. Incarnational ecclesiology, by contrast, tends to place greater value on pastoral skills and the ability to work with the local community. Of course, Incarnational Christians can benefit from good preaching, and Evangelical Christians need wise pastoral care. Nevertheless, since few potential priests have every desirable talent, bishops and those conducting selection on their behalf inevitably emphasize particular talents – and Evangelical and Incarnational emphases differ.

The present system, where there is a single central selection system, has frequently been criticized over the years for being confused in its criteria. Even if such criticisms are sometimes too strong, there is undoubtedly confusion amongst men and women contemplating ordination as to what is expected of them. This would be greatly eased by having two parallel systems of selection. Clearly the PEVs should supervise the selection of Incarnational candidates, with the help of those bishops in dioceses who are also giving Incarnational oversight.

There is no need formally to designate ordination-training courses as Evangelical or Incarnational.

Theological colleges and other training institutions have always tended to position themselves somewhere along the Evangelical/Incarnational spectrum. And most have altered their position from time to time in response to the changing demands of bishops and ordinands. As the parallel episcopates emerge, some institutions will doubtless remain manifestly Evangelical, and some may clearly identify with Incarnationalism. But it is possible – and surely desirable – that a few brave institutions may deliberately try to attract candidates from both parties.

So the ninth proposal is:

> *Evangelical and Incarnational bishops should establish separate systems for the selection of candidates for ordination.*

Concerning occasional offices

Evangelicals and Incarnationals have quite different attitudes to the "occasional offices," especially baptisms and weddings. Both, in their different ways, tend to bend, if not actually breach, the present laws relating to these offices.

Evangelical ecclesiology is inherently hostile to people without Christian commitment using baptism as a way of celebrating the arrival of a baby. And many Evangelicals are quite uneasy about infant baptism itself, preferring believer's baptism. As a result, Evangelical clergy often discourage people from exercising their legal right to have their babies baptized in the parish church. Indeed, there is now a widespread notion that many clergy "don't do christenings." Incarnational clergy by contrast welcome people exercising this right, because their ecclesiology is positive about rites of passage of all kinds. And, if they took their ecclesiology to its logical conclusions, they would experiment with other rituals to mark childbirth, in order to appeal more widely to modern sensibilities.

A similar divergence of attitudes exists towards weddings in church – although some Evangelical clergy regard church weddings between non-Christians as an opportunity for evangelism. There is, however, a further problem relating to marriages. Currently a couple can only be married in a particular church if one or both partners live in the parish or worship regularly in the church. The main historic reason for this rule appears to have been to prevent unseemly rivalry between clergy for weddings, and thence for the wedding fees. Yet today the important rivalry is not between one church and another, but between churches and other venues, including hotels and country houses. For Evangelicals, the main problem with the rule is that, if interpreted literally, it would prevent churchgoers' children, who have moved away, from being married in their parents' church. For Incarnationals the problem is far greater: their ecclesiology indicates that the church should actively compete with hotels and country houses, offering a better style of wedding than they can provide – yet the rule effectively gives hotels and country houses a free run. Incarnational ecclesiology also suggests that there should be more freedom in the form of weddings than the law relating to marriage in church currently allows.

The law relating to church marriages is currently under review, and the advent of parallel episcopates should obviously affect the reviewers' recommendations. In the meantime the bending of the rules should be tacitly tolerated. In regard to the location of weddings, the rules are contained in the Marriage Act 1949. While allowing people to marry at their "usual place of worship," it does not define what this means. More importantly, *Halsbury's Laws of England* makes clear that, even if this is interpreted extremely liberally, it does not affect the validity of the marriage.

Clearly many Incarnational clergy will want to add a further occasional office: the blessing of homosexual partnerships. It would be quite contrary to Incarnational ecclesiology to impose standard forms. Nonetheless it would probably be helpful if Incarnational bishops encouraged debate about appropriate words and symbols.

Thus the tenth proposal is:

> *It should be recognized that the rules relating to occasional offices are in various respects unsatisfactory for both Evangelicals and Incarnationals. In the short-term a very liberal interpretation of many of these rules should be tolerated. In the longer term the commission recommended above should consider appropriate changes.*

Concerning parochial democracy

The office of churchwarden is (according to Sidney and Beatrice Webb's *English Local Government*) the oldest democratically elected post in England, dating back at least to the 13th century. Every adult male resident of a parish was allowed both to vote and to stand. The principle of democracy was so ruthlessly applied that a man could be elected without his consent, and was then legally bound to serve. Churchwardens wielded considerable power over both the church itself and the civil life of the parish. Thus this historic office perfectly embodied Incarnational ecclesiology.

However, during the 20th century successive legislative changes gradually shifted the management of parish churches towards Evangelical ecclesiology – although, in fact, Anglo-Catholics were often the prime movers of these changes. In 1921 parochial church councils (PCCs) were given formal legal status (some parishes had already instituted them informally), and in 1956 most of the churchwardens' powers were transferred to the PCC – of which the churchwardens were ex officio members. The Synodical Government Measure 1969 laid down precise rules for the conduct of elections to the PCC. First, the electors should belong to the church electoral roll; and to join the electoral roll an individual must be baptized, and should declare in writing that he or she is a "member" of the Church of England (or belongs to a denomination in "communion" with it). Secondly, only those who are "communicant" members of the Church of England can be elected to the PCC.

Regarding the election of churchwardens, it remains the case that every adult resident of the parish, whose name appears on the local government register of electors, is entitled to vote. In addition, those on the church electoral roll as regular worshipers, but not resident in the parish, can vote. In general churchwardens should be on the electoral roll and also be communicants, but the bishop is allowed to waive these requirements. Thus with episcopal blessing the old system could still operate, in which the churchwarden could be anyone in the parish, elected by everyone. But, of course, the modern churchwarden has few powers beyond those vested in the PCC as a whole.

Manifestly this entire system is a mess, breaching two basic principles of democracy. First, there are two different electorates, one for PCC members and one for churchwardens, and yet churchwardens exercise their powers mainly as members of the PCC. Secondly, there are substantially different qualifications for electors and the elected, so that by no means all those on the electoral roll are eligible for election to the PCC. In practice many parishes ignore these problems (or are ignorant of them), electing both the churchwardens and the PCC at the annual general meeting of all those on the electoral roll, and allowing anyone on the electoral roll to stand.

The more serious difficulty is that the system frustrates the Incarnational impulse to integrate the church with the community. Since the rules, despite their messiness, are well suited to Evangelical churches, it would be wrong simply to discard them. And on the principle of minimizing short-term legislative changes, it would be a mistake to try and amend them. There is, however, a solution for Incarnational parishes within the present law. In essence it involves disbanding the PCC and replacing it with a charitable trust whose trustees are elected by the same people as elect the churchwardens. The churchwardens are ex officio trustees, and the Trust holds the church funds. Hence the churchwardens and other trustees work together in managing the church. There are two possible legal bases of this arrangement. First, according to section 84 of the Pastoral Measure 1983, if a parish fails to elect a PCC, its powers revert to the churchwardens. Secondly, the AGM can simply decide that the PCC should have only two members, who would automatically be the churchwardens.

Thus the eleventh proposal is:

> *Parishes under Incarnational episcopal oversight should be encouraged to disband their PCCs, and replace them with charitable trusts, whose trustees would consist of the churchwardens and others elected in the same way as the churchwardens. Incarnational bishops should as a matter of course exercise their right to waive the current restrictions on who may stand as churchwarden, allowing any adult living in a parish to stand.*

Concerning buildings

The Church of England has far more church buildings than it needs to accommodate its worshipers. This is especially true in the countryside, where most villages have a medieval church. But it is also true in inner cities where mock-Gothic edifices were built in Victorian times to provide spiritual accommodation for industrial workers and their families – but where the industries have now gone and the people moved away. It is doubtful whether the medieval rural churches or the Victorian urban churches were ever full. Wealthy landowners extended the rural church mainly to glorify God (and perhaps themselves as well), and wealthy industrialists with tender consciences greatly overestimated the devoutness of their employees. Today the ratio of worshipers to buildings is ludicrously low.

An important fact in the present success – or avoidance of failure – of Evangelicalism has been its determination to put worship before fabric. It has concentrated its efforts in relatively few buildings that are conveniently situated, drawing people from miles around, and it has adapted those buildings to suit the congregation's current spiritual needs. Yet the Church of England as a whole has been extremely reluctant to abandon buildings where the congregations are dwindling towards extinction. Instead, it has spread its clergy ever more thinly, so that in many rural areas today individual priests are struggling to maintain regular worship in five, ten or even a dozen separate churches; so they spend their Sundays dashing between them. And, of course, in such circumstances the quality of worship is hardly likely to attract newcomers.

If George Herbert were alive today, it is not hard to imagine what he would advocate. He would want to preserve the buildings as sacraments, and the local people to continue celebrating the popular festivals in them, as well as holding weddings and funerals. But he would urge the small minority wanting to worship Sunday by Sunday to travel to particular churches, so that the services may be truly worthy of God. My strong belief is that, if parishes were given the kind of freedom and changes in parochial government advocated earlier, then most of those parishes with very small congregations would sooner or later give up Sunday worship, and the parish as a whole would organize the celebration of the traditional festivals – perhaps inventing one or two "traditional" festivals of their own. Also by a kind of Darwinian process of selection certain churches would become the venues for Sundays.

There are two further related points to be made. First, it is far easier to raise money for maintaining buildings than for paying clergy. In villages with a fine medieval church the entire population is generally eager to preserve it. Indeed, people benefit directly by the effect that a well-kept church has on the local environment, and thence on house prices; and there are also substantial government subsidies for major works of repair. Secondly, if rural churches were kept unlocked during daylight hours, they would almost undoubtedly be used frequently for private reflection (which was one their main functions in medieval times), and would attract more tourists. There is evidence to suggest that church-going is more popular than it has ever been – but at times when services are *not* being held.

So the twelfth proposal is:

> *The Church of England as a whole should follow the successful Evangelical example of concentrating regular worship in relatively few churches, while at the same time encouraging smaller parishes to preserve their church buildings for their sacramental value, for private reflection, and for occasional corporate use.*

Concerning ecumenism

It is possible that parallel episcopates within the Church of England may make it possible to forge a new unity scheme with Methodism. English Methodists are divided along similar lines to Anglicans, although their debate has been more discreet and has attracted far less publicity. To my knowledge some Methodists of Incarnational convictions would be attracted by the idea of specifically Incarnational episcopal oversight, and I imagine there would be many

Evangelical Methodists who would happily accept an Evangelical episcopate.

The dramatic decline in the congregations of independent Evangelical churches has caused many within those churches to question the quality of their ministry. And they cannot help but be impressed by the quality of many of the ministers within Anglican Evangelical churches. The difference partly arises from the dramatic improvements that have occurred within Evangelical theological colleges, while most of the Bible colleges – where independent ministers are trained – remain comparatively dull and stodgy. A further problem for independent churches is that many men and women with appropriate spiritual gifts are deterred from entering ministry by the uncertainty of future employment. At present most independent Evangelicals continue to distrust the Church of England as an institution because in their view too many of the bishops are theologically unsound. But, if they could be certain of episcopal oversight by a bishop sympathetic to their convictions, many independent congregations might actually seek to join the Church of England – and thence enjoy the benefits of its superior ministry. Indeed, I know personally several congregations who, in the event of parallel episcopates, would be eagerly knocking at the Church of England's Evangelical door. And, if they were welcomed, their status would usually be that of a "daughter church" to an existing Anglican church.

For the foreseeable future the Church of England will remain wedded to its system of parishes, defined by lines on the map. A great portion of ecclesiastical law presumes the existence of geographical parishes, and to abandon the parochial system would involve a thorough going overhaul of the law, which cannot be an immediate prospect. However, in recent years some Evangelical churches have been bending the law by "planting" daughter churches within parishes where the ministry is not Evangelical. While this has caused some controversy and resentment, the parochial system has proved able to absorb it. Undoubtedly parallel episcopates will stimulate more church planting, as Evangelical churches create congregations in Incarnational parishes. And as independent Evangelical churches join the Church of England, this process will accelerate. If such a church happened to be within an Incarnational parish, it would become an instant plant.

Although Quakerism emerged in the 17th century in reaction to the apparent complacency of much Incarnational Anglicanism, Quakerism (at least within Britain) has gradually become highly Incarnational itself, and many Quakers are exemplars of Incarnational morality. Equally, many Incarnational Anglicans express admiration for Quakerism, and might even be tempted to join the Society of Friends, were it not for Quakerism's antipathy to any kind of symbolism or ritual. Although it would be impossible for there to be any kind of institutional unity between the Society and the Incarnational segment of the Church of England, a separate Incarnational episcopate will allow them to grow closer together in various informal ways. In the longer term one can imagine Incarnational

Anglicans forming similar links with the non-Christian religions that flourish in England, especially Hinduism and Sikhism that are themselves Incarnational in their theology.

So the thirteenth and final proposal is:

> *The Evangelicals and Incarnationals should take the opportunities that parallel episcopates afford to form closer bonds, and even merge with, other religious groups in England.*

AFTERWORD

I finished the first draft of this book at the beginning of December 2003, and then sent copies to seventy members of the Anglican Church, including archbishops, bishops, priests, theologians, churchwardens – and to lay-people who hold no office. And I tried to include all shades of Anglican opinion. I invited them to comment freely, expressing criticisms honestly and frankly.

The most frequent criticisms by far concern the way in which I describe the main traditions within Anglicanism. Some people, who fall into the Incarnational camp, feel that most Incarnationals are more firmly tied to biblical teaching than I seem to suggest. Others in the Evangelical camp think that I over-emphasize the theological importance of the Evangelical revival in the 18th century, arguing that there is greater continuity between early Puritanism and present Evangelical thought. But somewhat to my surprise all my respondents seem happy with the view that Anglican history should be interpreted in terms of two parties – rather than the three parties that used to figure prominently in books on Anglicanism. And none refutes the contention that it is the Incarnationals, not the Evangelicals, who have changed their theological and moral position in recent decades, and that this change underlies the present crisis.

I expected that some would bridle at the term "Incarnational" for one of these parties. In fact, amongst those choosing to comment, everyone is favorable, and some are positively enthusiastic. People did, however, raise two major difficulties with "Evangelical." The first is that a significant and growing number of people regarded as Evangelical want to drop the term. This is because they regard their beliefs as straightforwardly orthodox, and as standing firmly in the center of traditional Anglican teaching. The second difficulty, which is closely related, is that many people who would not be regarded as Evangelical – nor would they regard themselves as such – nonetheless share the basic Evangelical epistemology, and so are closely aligned with Evangelicals on matters of theology and morality. These include most, but by no means all, of those usually described as "Anglo-Catholic." In the light of these difficulties I have amended the first section of Chapter 1, suggesting that the Eames Commission might prefer to adopt the name "Orthodox" – though I explain why in this book I have stuck with "Evangelical."

The bulk of my respondents' comments concern the central theme of this book, that in some Anglican provinces there should be distinct episcopal arrangements for each party. The great majority is favorable, agreeing that this is the only practical means of preventing outright schism. Indeed, I have been impressed that leaders on both sides support this idea. It should be said that some, particularly on the Incarnational side, express regret that distinct episcopal arrangements have become necessary. Also a leading theologian made the point that each side is quite diverse within itself in its views and attitudes. But he recognizes that a point comes when a coalition cannot hold together as a single entity, and that this point has now been reached with Anglicanism as a whole – so some degree of separation between the two sides, along the lines proposed in this book, is inevitable.

Two respondents, while supportive in general terms, expressed practical concerns. A leading gay activist within the Church of England is critical of the idea that the "default" position for a parish is that it is unwilling to have a priest in a homosexual partnership, since this effectively concedes that mainstream Anglicanism is now Evangelical, which he disputes. He would prefer the default position to be the other way round. In my view this is not only legally problematic, as I explained in the relevant section, but also fails to recognize that opposition to priests in homosexual partnerships is the historic norm within Anglicanism. A prominent historian of Christian art expressed concern that even in a pro-gay parish an Evangelical minority could effectively scupper any attempt to come out on the Incarnational side. In strictly constitutional terms this is wrong, since in a vote on the matter the majority would prevail. Yet, as I recognized earlier, people in such parishes may baulk at the prospect of conflict amongst themselves, and try to avoid it by remaining in the default position.

Two more general concerns are raised by Archbishop Idowu-Fearon in his Foreword; and other respondents have expressed these in various ways. The first is that, once the two sides have separate episcopates, they may drift apart more rapidly than they have been already. The second is that the Incarnationals, left to their own devices, may lack moral and spiritual discipline, and become corrupt and decadent. The Archbishop's foreword prompted me to write the tenth proposal in Chapter 1.

A few of my respondents, however, are firmly opposed to any kind of separate episcopal arrangements. In fact, eight out of the seventy are. And the reasons for their opposition merit careful consideration.

The first reason, expressed by two Evangelicals, is that those regarding homosexual partnerships as morally acceptable are heretical, and should be subject to discipline. Thus not only should men and women in homosexual partnerships be debarred from the ordained ministry, but also heterosexuals speaking openly in favor of such partnerships should be officially reprimanded – and, if they persist, should also be debarred. Incarnationals should be wary of dismissing this view as bigotry or homophobia, since it is the logical outcome of Evangelical epistemology. In the present context the important question is how strongly this view is held. If Evangelicals as a whole regard it as non-negotiable, then schism is inevitable. But my own impression is that most Evangelical Anglicans across the world are anxious to maintain some kind of unity, and are willing to make compromises to this end. Thus I am confident that the proposals contained in this book, after considerable argument amongst Evangelicals, would carry the great majority.

The second reason, expressed by an Incarnational bishop, is that we should rather strive for reconciliation in the present dispute. In his view having separate episcopal arrangements would institutionalize division rather than overcome it. In *The Way Forward* Stephen Sykes makes an important distinction between personal and doctrinal reconciliation. It is a matter of Christian discipleship, to which Evangelicals and Incarnationals alike are bound, that we should treat those with differing views from our own with courtesy and respect. Stephen Sykes pleads for more effort in practicing those virtues. But reconciliation between doctrines that are logically opposed to one another is impossible – a point on which Evangelicals seem entirely clear. The question, therefore, is what nature and degree of doctrinal difference makes belonging to the same religious institution impossible. Clearly we regard the doctrinal differences between Christianity and Islam as so great that they must remain institutionally separate – even though it is vital for the future of global civilization that Christians and Muslims are mutually courteous and respectful. On the other hand, Roman Catholicism is able to maintain sufficient doctrinal homogeneity to remain institutionally unified – albeit by means of an authoritarian structure that most Anglicans would regard as unacceptable. The argument of this book is that modern Anglicanism lies between these two poles: that some degree of separateness is necessary, but that both sides stand to benefit by remaining within a single over-arching structure.

The third reason, expressed by Bishop Michael Ingham in his Foreword, is that many Anglicans do not easily fit into either of the two parties that I have described; and he says that many in his own diocese would call themselves as "evangelical-incarnationalists" or vice-versa. In purely logical terms it is impossible to belong to both parties according to the definition I gave in Chapter 1, since their epistemologies are mutually exclusive. Nonetheless, as I also indicated in Chapter 1, many people feel drawn in both directions. This is why the issue of homosexuality is so important, functioning as – in Bishop Michael's words – "the tip of the iceberg." If you are truly Evangelical, in the sense that you regard the Bible as the unique and complete divine revelation, then you cannot help but regard homosexual sex as profoundly sinful. Hence you would not, and should not, accept the ministry of a priest in such a homosexual partnership. Conversely, if you regard experience as authoritative, then, in the light of modern empirical understanding of homosexuality, you would be inclined to look favorably on homosexual partnerships, and so would be quite happy to accept the ministry of a priest, bishop or archbishop who had a homosexual partner.

The fourth reason, expressed by a church historian, is that the present dominance of Evangelicalism may prove to be temporary, and hence the present opposition to homosexual clergy and bishops may be short-lived. He even believes that, if the present pope has a more liberal successor, this will stimulate liberal Anglo-Catholicism (with which he identifies) into fresh vigor, and it may replace Evangelicalism as the main influence in Anglican affairs. He hopes that the Eames Commission will produce a "fudge" that will allow things to carry on as they are now. While it is conceivable that within England Evangelicalism may eventually wane, this is surely highly unlikely within the Anglican Church as a whole, where in most provinces

Evangelicals have always dominated. Besides, such speculation is hardly relevant to the present crisis. There is ample evidence that, if the Eames Commission comes up with nothing substantial, then Evangelicals will take matters into their own hands, bringing about an extremely messy *de facto* schism. Indeed, that already appears to be happening in the USA. The bitterness and ill will generated by such an outcome, and the damage caused to the image of Anglicanism, would be far worse than the schism itself.

The fifth reason, expressed by Bishop Michael Ingham and by an English Incarnation bishop, is that separate Episcopal arrangements for those favorable to homosexual priests and bishops would set a dangerous precedent, encouraging any group with a strongly-held view to demand its own episcopacy. Indeed, the separate arrangements for those opposed to women priests are serving as a precedent for the proposals in this book, thereby seeming to confirm how easy it is to slip down the slope into institutional chaos. In my view this is the most serious objection of all, and I did not give it proper attention in the first draft of this book. As a result I have added a ninth proposal to Chapter 1, which answers this objection in detail.

Books about Anglicanism used to praise its comprehensiveness, and this quality was one of the main reasons why I became Anglican after my conversion to Christianity in 1970. If there is a schism, then neither side will be able to claim to be comprehensive. The theme of this book is that in the present circumstances Anglicanism can only remain comprehensive by also becoming more flexible than its present structures allow. Although political analogies may be dubious, it is worth remembering that Britain, unlike most other countries, has avoided bloody revolutions in recent centuries through the flexibility of its political institutions, which have allowed diverse interests and attitudes to be accommodated. My hope and plea is that Anglicanism may avoid its own bloody revolution by similar means.